Solution Focused Therapy
for the Helping Professions

of related interest

A Guide to Psychological Debriefing
Managing Emotional Decompression and Post-Traumatic Stress Disorder
David Kinchin
Foreword by Professor Gordon Turnbull
ISBN 978 1 84310 492 6

Working with Suicidal Individuals
A Guide to Providing Understanding, Assessment and Support
Tony White
ISBN 978 1 84905 115 6

Introduction to Counselling Survivors of Interpersonal Trauma
Christiane Sanderson
ISBN 978 1 84310 962 4

Counselling Survivors of Domestic Abuse
Christiane Sanderson
ISBN 978 1 84310 606 7

Therapeutic Journal Writing
An Introduction for Professionals
Kate Thompson
Foreword by Kathleen Adams
ISBN 978 1 84310 690 6
Writing for Therapy or Personal Development Series

Reflective Practice in Mental Health
Advanced Psychosocial Practice with Children, Adolescents and Adults
Edited by Martin Webber and Jack Nathan
Foreword by Alan Rushton
ISBN 978 1 84905 029 6
Reflective Practice in Social Care

Promoting Psychological Well-Being in Children with Acute and Chronic Illness
Melinda Edwards and Penny Titman
ISBN 978 1 84310 967 9

Solution Focused Therapy for the Helping Professions

Barry Winbolt

Jessica Kingsley Publishers
London and Philadelphia

Epigraph from Gingerich 2010 on p.19 is reproduced by permission of Wally Gingerich. Exercise from Freedman and Combs 1996 on pp.98–99 is adapted by permission of W.W. Norton.

First published in 2011
by Jessica Kingsley Publishers
116 Pentonville Road
London N1 9JB, UK
and
400 Market Street, Suite 400
Philadelphia, PA 19106, USA

www.jkp.com

Library of Congress Cataloging in Publication Data
Winbolt, Barry, 1946-
Solution focused therapy for the helping professions / Barry Winbolt.
  p. cm.
Includes bibliographical references and index.
ISBN 978-1-84310-970-9 (alk. paper)
1. Solution-focused brief therapy. 2. Counselor and client. 3. Counseling. I. Title.
RC489.S65W56 2011
616.89'147--dc22
                    2010028489

British Library Cataloguing in Publication Data
A CIP catalogue record for this book is available from the British Library

ISBN 978 1 84310 970 9

Printed and bound in Great Britain by
MPG Books Group

For Michelle, with love

Contents

Introduction

Practitioners in many fields are these days using therapeutic techniques in their work. Social and community workers, teachers, nurses, occupational therapists and speech and language therapists and many more are reliant on communication and other skills drawn from the counselling professions when interacting with their client groups. These professions and many others – broadly characterised as the 'helping professions' – need their communications to be effective and empowering to their clients, but at the same time respectful and creative.

This book will tell you all you need to know to be able to start using the techniques of Solution Focused Brief Therapy (SFBT) in your work. It covers the essential points of the approach, presented in a way that has been developed in my therapy practice and during my training workshops around the UK and Europe. It is intended to give enough of an explanation of what SFBT is about for you to start thinking about how you work with people in a totally new way. If you are already familiar with SFBT this book can be used as a revision guide.

Such a summary must by definition leave out a lot of material. SFBT evolved out of a rich and innovative history. The pioneers of the approach have proved themselves to be among the most creative and able minds in psychology and psychotherapy. What I offer here is a starting point and I urge you – if you are serious about wanting to be more effective in your work – to read a good deal more about the subject once you have absorbed these ideas. I have included a recommended reading list and other resources at the end of the book. I would also advise you to see as many people working as possible by attending workshops and conferences.

The following pages owe much to contributors who will never be named. They are the people who have attended my workshops and seminars and with whom I have been able to discuss these ideas. They come from such a wide range of occupations that it would be impractical to list them in detail here. A summary includes professionals from the social, health and welfare sectors, from education, pastoral care and the police. I have also presented these ideas to lawyers, military personnel, business consultants, vets, dentists, priests and many others. The levels of enthusiasm and engagement shown for these ideas by such diverse and experienced groups of people have proved to me the wide ranging value of this approach. Being able to air the ideas in this way enabled me to clarify my thinking about the process in general and also – and perhaps more important – to consider many ways of putting the ideas across to people who, for the most part, were coming fresh to the subject (and occasionally sceptical about its usefulness as well). This has been an enormous help to me in ways that simply working as a therapist, however much feedback I got from my clients, would never have provided. I must also acknowledge the many professionals, whom I count both as colleagues and teachers, who I have been lucky enough to meet and discuss ideas with.

Not that I wish to neglect my clients, who are after all central to the process of therapy as well as the development and maturation of any therapist. I often think of clients as 'seeds' in what they bring to the equation when they enter the therapeutic relationship. Thinking about it now, I realise that they also helped germinate something in me that continues to develop, helped along by our discussions and our successes together.

If I have brought anything to the process it has been the way I present these ideas, but they are not my ideas. I have to pay tribute to the greats of SFBT, and indeed psychology in general, those I know personally and those I have only met through their writing and training events. If you find these ideas interesting, I encourage you to get to know them too.

Terminology

Since Solution Focused Brief Therapy (SFBT) uses the terminology of therapy, I do the same. I have opted for the terms 'therapist', 'helper' or 'practitioner' and 'client' or 'service user' for convenience. These are terms of convenience, not an attempt to reframe all helping as therapy. You may not think of the relationship between yourself and those you work with in these terms so I hope that you can make the necessary allowances. All relationships which require problem-solving or personal development strategies can benefit when guided by solution focused (SF) thinking.

The term client refers to the person traditionally known as the patient in healthcare settings. Sometimes therapists are required to work with clients who are referred by a third party or agency: an employer, the courts or social services for example. Even though other agencies may be calling the shots or even paying the therapist's fees or salary, I always refer to the other individual in the therapeutic consultation or helping relationship as the client.

I use the term 'therapist' and 'helper' to mean anyone in the healing or helping role. Many people who work in professions involving support, guidance or education may fulfil a therapeutic role but do not necessarily think of themselves in those terms. The ideas described in this book will nevertheless be of value.

To clarify this a little further, I am using the term therapy as shorthand for all forms of psychotherapy and counselling, and any other relationship which could be deemed 'healing' in its widest sense: to influence a person's sense of well-being. Jerome and Julia Frank, in their classic *Persuasion and Healing* (1991), say that such influence is characterised by:

a) A healing agent, i.e. the person or group in the role of helper who may or may not be professionally trained in that role

b) A sufferer who seeks relief from a)

c) A healing relationship...where influence is exercised primarily by words, acts and rituals in which sufferer and healer participate jointly. (Frank and Frank 1991, p.2)

Many professional relationships could declare the aim of 'influencing a person's sense of well-being' and so come easily within this definition. This is borne out by the increasing interest in SFBT from groups who do not normally describe themselves as therapists (for example, in social work, education, human resources, the voluntary sector and prisons).

Some people refer to SFBT as a 'model of therapy' but I do not think this is helpful. People get very attached to their particular models and it has been my experience that the quickest way to alienate someone is to tell them that there is a new model they must adopt. I prefer to think about the ideas outlined here as a way of thinking, or a way of talking to people; a language. Furman and Ahola describe it as 'a conversation dominated by "solution-talk"' (1992), and I think this is an apt description. Experience has shown me that many people find this easier to digest (and to integrate into their way of working) than the idea of a model, which after all amounts to a belief system. As we are all too often reminded, people will go to extremes to protect their beliefs. Even highly trained professionals are susceptible to this, which is probably what led two of the most informed SFBT practitioners in the world to comment 'Our experience has always been (that) those students *least* burdened with abstract theoretical notions are usually the *most* capable of learning solution focused therapy and, for that matter, therapy skills in general.' (Berg and Miller, 1992 p.1).

CHAPTER 1

The Helping Professions

This book is aimed specifically at people whose work involves helping others in some capacity. In recent years the term 'helping professions' has come to be used to describe those of us whose work involves helping people tackle some aspect of their lives that has become problematic (e.g. Barsky 2000; Combs 1971).

Some occupations are formally recognised as part of the helping professions by virtue of the fact that their daily work involves supporting people, for example, social work, counselling, psychiatry and the clergy. But there is a second group, much larger and covering many more professions, where the primary role is not seen as caring or support in the same way, but where the daily routine will inevitably involve helping people in crisis or distress, or who are struggling with the effects of social deprivation or health-related problems, or helping people to adapt to dramatic change in their lives.

This army of 'informal helpers' uses many of the same skills as the first group – essentially these are the skills of counselling – yet they will often receive little or no training to develop their helping skills because the 'supporting' aspects of their work are seen as secondary or incidental to their primary role (Egan 1994).

This second group includes staff in callings as diverse as advocacy, charity and aid work, conflict resolution, human resources, the law, medicine, occupational health, probation, physiotherapy, social work, human resources, teaching and many others. Many of these professions use counselling and therapeutic approaches in their practice, and those which do not at least use the skills of counselling such as rapport-building, the conscious use of empathy, listening, questioning, problem-solving and supporting. Some also make use of supervision, where a more experienced professional 'de-briefs' the practitioner at regular intervals, to aid personal development, safeguard professional standards and support the worker (Egan 1998; Hawkins and Shohet 2000).

One thing that all those who work in the helping professions have in common is that they talk to those they help. Counsellors and psychotherapists do talking therapy, but while everyone who supports or cares for others has the opportunity to use language creatively and therapeutically, few are exposed to training that will help them do it effectively. This book sets out to address this by offering a Solution Focused Brief Therapy (SFBT) framework for the helping professions.

There is a third group where these skills are just as important but who receive neither recognition nor training to support them in their helping role. Almost six million carers in the UK provide unpaid care for a family member, friend or partner who is ill, frail or disabled (DOH 2009). Though not formally part of the helping professions, in supporting those they care for they need to use the same skills of communication, problem-solving, listening, persuading and influencing as any of their professional counterparts. Frequently this role is even more arduous than that of the professional helper because carers provide round-the-clock support for those they care for, and many are also in full- or part-time work.

The role of helper

Whether paid or voluntary, through a combination of personal qualities, skills and the helping relationship, members of the helping professions seek to enhance the quality of peoples' lives by producing growth conditions leading to positive outcomes that are important to the client (Brammer and MacDonald 1999). This usually means that in addition to supporting their clients, helpers also help them to learn or develop skills that will enable them to become partially or wholly independent of the helper. Helpers therefore have a primary goal to 'Help clients manage their problems in living more effectively and develop unused or underused opportunities more fully' (Egan 1998, p.7).

Clients also have desired outcomes or goals. Often these may not be explicit at the outset, they simply want support or relief from some problem or distress. While many helpers see supporting others as a key part of their role, so is guiding the client towards increased self-sufficiency or independence. Once the initial level of support has been established, and this is usually a by-product of a healthy helping relationship, the two work collaboratively to define some workable goals for the client, and then help them move towards them.

In recent years the helping relationship has been subtly but persistently shifting from one where the emphasis was on support to one where client independence is becoming the order of the day. Empathetic and caring support is still fundamental, but in our target-driven age of financial pressure and reduced resources, this independence is increasingly a primary role of agencies and services in the social health and welfare sectors.

For the past twenty years I have been involved, as a consultant, trainer and therapist, in helping teams and individuals to make this transition. Faced with the need to cut costs staff have been told they must 'work smarter'. Though some people resist this trend it is inexorable. In some cases helping professionals feel that they are being pressured into working more briefly with their clients and in some quarters this leads to considerable tension, not to say foot-dragging and occasional refusal to adopt new practices. In my experience this initial and understandable resistance is easily overcome when practitioners realise that becoming more effective in their work with their clients in no way compromises the quality of the service they offer, on the contrary clients are happier, helpers are more energised and interventions are usually briefer.

Problems are the starting point for the helping process. Problem situations arise inside ourselves, between ourselves and others, within families, groups, teams and organisations, at work and in communities. Those we help, whether they are troubled by intrapersonal problems, unwanted habits or behaviour, or something external to themselves such as relationship difficulties, unfair treatment, navigating complex administrations, finding their voice or becoming more effective in some aspect of their lives, seek improvement in some way (Egan 1998). They are seeking to change something about themselves or in their relationships with others and they are seeking – or have been told they must seek – help to alleviate their difficulties and become more effective.

The role of the helper to is to fulfil two major purposes; establishing a relationship and facilitating action (Brammer and MacDonald 1999). Incumbent in this role is the responsibility to those we help to be as effective and resourceful as we can in our helping, which in turn implies a commitment to continuing professional development to enhance our skills and understanding. If we do not do the best we can by continuing to learn and improve we are failing ourselves and our clients.

Implicit too in the role of helper is the ability to help clients solve problems. Most of us are not very well schooled in doing this, and many helping professionals struggle with this aspect of their work. Most have studied models of helping, but these often prove inappropriate or ill-adapted to the complexities of our clients' worlds, their lack of motivation and even, at times, their hostility. SFBT provides a structured, short-term approach which enables client and helper to establish a collaborative relationship, plan actions and construct solutions to their problems.

Solution-talk versus problem-talk

SFBT is an approach to therapeutic communications that empowers both clients and helpers. Though it has developed – as its title suggests – as a form of brief, talking therapy, the approach brings with it a wealth of easily learned and adaptable techniques which will enhance the skills of any capable health professional whatever the setting.

Traditionally clinical approaches have focused on what is wrong with the client, communications have naturally followed suit. But imagine for a moment a world where, in discussing a problem with the client, rather than focusing on what is wrong and exploring the problem, we focus on what is working; on the successes and strengths which the client (and helping professionals very often too) will have overlooked.

Steve de Shazer, generally credited with being the originator of the approach, says: 'Traditionally therapy focused on problem-solving... when solution focused, the therapist talks about changes, differences that make a difference and solutions, rather than talking about difficulties, complaints and problems' (1986, pp.48–9). The changes that clients experience simply as a result of this cognitive shift in focus can be quite remarkable, and therapists and helpers find the approach feeds their enthusiasm for working with their clients, rather than depleting their energy in hours spent discussing the problem.

Over the years the thousands of helping professionals I have met through my workshops and seminars have confirmed the appeal of introducing solution focused ideas into their work. Many of these were counsellors who were seeking to refresh or update their skills, but most have been from other professions, and who felt the need to develop the skills that would enable them to work more effectively with their clients.

Sometimes this was because in the increasingly 'results-driven' culture of the public services their caseload was increasing, while others were seeking to improve their work-related communication skills. Whatever the reason, all were agreed that they wanted to work more effectively in helping their clients.

Why the helping professions need SFBT

A few years ago a physiotherapist said to me, 'I never wanted to be a counsellor, but as soon as I saw my first client I realised that was part of what I have to do.' Since then I have repeatedly heard similar comments from practitioners from many different backgrounds in the social, health and welfare fields, education, the church, occupational health and, increasingly lately, in business as well.

The role of the helping professional requires a full and effective range of communications skills. Just as a physiotherapist's role – whether hospital based or out in the community – means working with people who may be anywhere on the spectrum from contented and cooperative to angry and antisocial, so many other professionals, from teachers to social workers, acupuncturist to medical practitioner, find their communication skills tested to the limit in demanding situations.

This does not only mean service users. Relatives, other carers and even colleagues can test our abilities (and our nerves) to the limit at times. The ability to communicate as an effective professional is part of the remit of virtually every carer, helper and support worker. Even though most of the people that I have met in almost two decades spent training healthcare staff have shown themselves to be capable and dynamic in this area, I also meet those who admit to feeling drained, demoralised or at least defeated by a client or patient's non-compliance, inability or unwillingness to follow instructions, or their constant negativity.

Dealing with people in such circumstances means having to handle the full range of emotional expressions and experiences which, though they might be quite incidental to the main object of the relationship, can make the difference between success or failure. And success or failure will have a critical impact on outcome and thereby on the professional self-esteem, confidence and morale of the helper. We can't win 'em all, as they say, but every successful and satisfying outcome breathes a little bit of new life into us and benefits our future clients.

So how would it be to feel more confident and resourceful in the face of even the most daunting response from a patient or client? The benefits for service users and practitioners could be enormous. SFBT gives us a range of tools to do just that and more.

CHAPTER 2

The Solution Focused
Approach

Solution Focused Brief Therapy is a short-term goal-focused therapeutic approach which helps clients change by constructing solutions rather than dwelling on problems. Elements of the desired solution often are already present in the client's life, and become the basis for ongoing change. The therapist intervenes only to the extent necessary, with treatment usually lasting for less than six sessions. (Gingerich 2010)

Solution Focused Brief Therapy (SFBT from here on) is one of a family of approaches, known as a systemic therapies, that have been developed over the past fifty years or so, first in the USA, and eventually evolving around the world, including Europe. The title SFBT, and the specific steps involved in its practice, are attributed to Steve de Shazer and his team at the Brief Family Therapy Family Center in Milwaukee. Their work in the early 1980s built on that of a number of other innovators, among them Milton Erickson, and the group at the Mental Research Institute (MRI) at Palo Alto – Gregory Bateson, Don Jackson, Paul Watzlawick, John Weakland, Virginia Satir, Jay Haley and others. All these names are important, not just as pioneers of a new way of doing therapy but also because their various collaborations and writings represent nothing short of a revolution in the way we think about social and mental health and well-being. Systemic approaches are now in constant demand. Their efficacy is well established and supported by a solid and ever increasing body of research. Solution focused thinking has earned its place and is widely accepted in the fields of therapy, social care, education and business.

The steps involved in SFBT – which are easy to learn, if a little more difficult to perfect in practice – can be viewed as a paradigm, a way of thinking or even a language. Using these steps means understanding the organising principles, developing the habit of using the main tools and above all being comfortable in the role where you use them, be it as therapist, teacher, social worker or any one of the many other professions that have learned the benefit of working in a solution focused way.

A traditional focus

Traditionally, our attempts at problem-solving revolve around analysis, as if, in searching diligently for the cause, we will find an answer to the problem. This in itself generates a number of problems:

1. Analysis is about thinking. Most problems require action, doing something, to fix or work round them. Thinking is fine, but not all thinking is equally valid in problem-solving.

2. Clients are often already very adept at analysis and rumination (less so at reflection, of which more later). When they seek professional help it is to do something different. We would be failing them if all we do with them is more analysis and encourage rumination. They can do this perfectly well and on their own time and without the help of a professional.

3. Analysis looks for cause. Therapeutic interventions deal with effect. Most people understand that we cannot change the past (where the cause occurred). They are more interested in having something better happen from now on (Yapko 1992).

SFBT provides a way out of these and other dilemmas. It provides a well-established method that is effective, more empowering to the client and energising for the person in the role of helper, advisor or therapist. Rather than examining their inner world, thoughts and feelings and past events, SFBT focuses on three main areas in the client's life:

- their abilities and strengths
- the present and the future
- their achievements and successes.

Since SFBT encourages a practical, active and 'how to' stance in seeking solutions rather than a theory-driven analysis of problems, becoming solution focused requires a shift in thinking. For some people in training this seems to be the most difficult part. If you have been schooled to look for the whys and wherefores rather than seeking out what is working and doing more of it, SFBT can seem strange, and some people fail to see how uncluttered the approach is. When learning something new it requires a leap of faith to embrace the new ideas and a different way of doing things. If you are new to this approach, or uncertain about how to integrate it more fully into your way of working, I encourage you to familiarise yourself with the SFBT literature, transcripts and workshops – exposure to this way of thinking is the quickest way to start learning the new language and thinking habits – and then to start using it. Like any language, new skill or habit, practice breeds ability and confidence.

A solution orientation

Thinking about and discussing the outcomes we want, rather than seeking to understand the cause of the problem initially seems odd to those of us who have been taught – by education or society – to look for the weak points in an argument, seek out fault, attribute cause or commiserate about our problems. SFBT does not see these as a necessary part of the route to deciding goals and moving towards solutions.

One of the fathers of the field, Bill O'Hanlon, describes it as 'A new way to think about and approach therapy'. He adds: 'It is a method that focuses on people's competence rather than their deficits, their strengths rather than their weaknesses, their possibilities rather than their limitations' (O'Hanlon and Weiner-Davis 1989, p.xx). So we tend to speak about success, rather than failure, exceptions to the problem rather than the problem itself and where the client wants to go (their goals) rather than their history.

SFBT is a collaborative and creative process requiring the expertise of both participants (or all of them when working with a group or family). The 'Solution' in the title refers to the direction we are going in; we remain *oriented towards* solutions, as opposed to the traditional tendency of directing our attention to the problem. Finding out what the client wants to change in their lives and negotiating a course of action that is acceptable to them enables solutions to be constructed. Information and ideas about how to go about it arise as a product of the conversation. This is a critical point. If the solutions were already apparent, either our clients or those around them would have spotted them. The major strength of this approach is that it identifies and amplifies client skills and resources, empowering them to think about their goals. By working collaboratively client and therapist are far more resourceful and productive than either would be working alone. Solutions are thus 'co-created'. Since creativity cannot be rehearsed in advance, in SFBT we steer clear of the temptation to imagine and answer questions before they arise, as this tends to result in 'That would never work because…' type of thinking. In other words, SFBT works by doing it, not mentally rehearsing it.

I mention this because a point has frequently been raised in my workshops along the lines of 'Ah well, this is all well and good with other people's clients, but I could never talk about solutions to my clients. Their particular problems have no solutions.' They then go on to talk about the intractable social difficulties that their clients are typically enmeshed in, or that they work, for example, with the terminally ill. Such thinking on the part of the therapist is a product of problem focused thinking which misses the point: we do not know what is possible for our client until we discuss it with them. Therapy is more productive when it focuses on the impact of the difficulties (or diagnosis), rather than attempting to change the circumstances themselves.

Discussing problem-free times and successes is just the start in a process that is as empowering for the client as it can be liberating for the therapist. True collaboration is fascinating, enjoyable and full of surprises. It requires diligence on the part of the therapist and genuine curiosity if we are to help the client uncover resources they have hitherto missed (they can't tell us about them if they haven't noticed them). The creative use of questions is fundamental to the approach, so is astute observation and a genuine belief that the process can help people change their lives for the better. Questions are a powerful and generally under-used device. Influence is an unavoidable part of every human interaction. SFBT uses both intentionally to achieve its purpose.

The solution focused conversation

In summary, people familiar with using SFBT see the future not as a fixed and immutable destiny but as negotiable space laced with possibilities. Having solution focused conversations with our clients involves the creative use of questions to discover what is working in their lives, as a starting point to producing change. This means looking for exceptions to the problem; times when it is absent or goes unnoticed, and times when they function well despite the problem. Identifying 'problem free' times in this way demonstrates to the client that their difficulties are not as all encompassing as they had believed. The result can be an empowering change of perspective which itself generates further change.

Such conversations are marked by genuine curiosity, warmth, respect and humour on the part of the therapist. They presuppose success and work to demonstrate to the client that they are a resourceful human being who, however serious their setbacks or situation, has more going for them than is stacked against them.

To these ends SFBT provides a number of simple and highly effective tools aimed at helping the client view their situation more resourcefully. These encourage strategic thinking and promote the development of life skills, enabling a change in their perceptions and how they interact with the world. In effect, he or she can become more skilful in navigating their way through their life and dealing with the inevitable challenges, setbacks and tests that are a part of living.

Steve de Shazer, generally claimed to be the originator of the approach, asks us to envisage an experiment: 'Imagine that you have spent the last half hour talking to Mr A about all the problems in his life, focusing particularly on his feelings of depression. How do you feel after that half hour?' When I use this in my workshops participants tell me that, in part one of the exercise, details pile up, negativity increases and the result is that very soon they can't see the wood for the trees. The result for the 'therapist' is feeling overwhelmed, confused and at times even hopeless. As de Shazer says, 'If this is the way the therapists feel, can you imagine what the client must feel like?'

For the second part of the experiment he asks us to 'Imagine that you have spent the last half hour talking to Mr B about all the things that have gone well in his life, focusing particularly on his feelings of success. How do you feel after that half hour?' (de Shazer 1994, pp.66–7). Here the people in my workshops tell me that things feel lighter, they discover strengths and resources they never knew the client had and the likelihood of moving forward seems more tangible and real, and the whole experience is motivating and stimulating.

Working in a solution focused way does not mean searching for some solution to clients' ills. Rather it is that conversations are oriented towards some sort of positive outcome (or goal), albeit within the very real constraints some clients face. A critical part of the exercise is to have the client define their own goals. Many, if not all, will need help with this, but providing that the therapist's approach is duly sensitive and creative most will be able to do it with a little encouragement. As de Shazer says,

'When solution focused, the therapist talks about changes, differences that make a difference and solutions, rather than talking about difficulties, complaints and problems.' The changes that some clients experience simply as a result of this cognitive shift can be quite remarkable.

The following transcript is of a first session using basic SFBT techniques. Susanne is a divorcee in late middle age. At her intake discussion she spoke about relationship difficulties, poor sleep patterns and rumination. She is in remission from cancer. During her illness, she received counselling and had good emotional support from colleagues.

Introduction

Therapist: This is our first session, so what brings you here?

Susanne: Um, well, feeling I just feel that I've made a big mess of a lot of my life and I feel kind of guilty about it, paralysed and sort of ruminating a lot on the past, going over and over things and not really knowing what to do next.

Therapist: So you'd like to break that pattern or do something different about that?

Susanne: Yes.

Therapist: So, in an ideal world, when we've finished working together, what would be different?

Susanne: I wouldn't spend many hours of the day thinking about the past, going over and over events.

Therapist: So, you'd be doing something different, if you wouldn't be thinking about the past, what *would* you be doing?

Susanne: I'd be more motivated to do things that I *think* I'm interested in. I say *think* I'm interested in because a lot of the time I'm not even sure what I *am* interested in.

Therapist: OK. Can I check if I've understood it then? There's this process of rumination that kind of takes you over to a point where it actually eclipses other things, it keeps stopping you even exploring other avenues. So you spoke about being paralysed by it so that you have lost your motivation? (*Preliminary definition of the problem*)

Susanne: Yes.

Therapist:	And yet I know from our brief discussion the other day that you actually have a pretty active life, and you've done lots of things. (*Search for successes and other resources*)
Susanne:	Yes, on paper I've had a fabulous life. Even now, when I go out, I do laugh a lot. I've got friends, and my brother is so funny, and in fact probably one of my best friends. (*Exceptions to the problem*)
Therapist:	OK.
Susanne:	And every day I have to admit I do have high moments and I think, yes, my life's been pretty good actually.
Therapist:	You have high moments every day?
Susanne:	Yes, they don't last long but I would say I do. (*Confirmation of exceptions*)

Commentary

A few minutes into the session we have established what Susanne says the problem is, and that, despite the pervasive nature of her rumination and feelings of guilt, these are balanced by, so far unexplored, positive aspects of her life.

Looking for resources

Therapist:	So, to complete the background a bit, you were married for several years, you have two children together, who I believe are now in successful careers. You now live alone, and have a good social life. You also told me that you like your job.
Susanne:	Yes, but, I was never happy with my husband. Never. It was never really that great. And I had a number of affairs when I was married because he was always away a lot and it was remarkably easy, but I didn't really like living like that, so eventually…
Therapist:	…When you say 'like that', what do you mean? With that sort of dishonesty in the relationship?
Susanne:	Yes, with that kind of dishonesty in the relationship, I didn't like it but I hadn't got the guts to leave until the children

were quite grown up. Then I did leave. But I left and I went to live with a man who turned out to be completely bonkers really. He turned out to have a lot of addiction problems and he's violent and I got myself out of that.

Therapist: And, time scale? You were married for how many years?

Susanne: I was married for 23 years, and that ended almost four years ago.

Therapist: OK.

Susanne: And then I lived with this other man, who turned out to be unliveable with, for about 19 months, and that was traumatic really, we had to get the police involved to get rid of him. Then as soon as I'd sort of got myself out of all that, I felt well maybe things were going to be OK, but I got involved with this young Egyptian man, who I met here in Britain but I went to Egypt with him. Again, found out that he was, well, a liar and a cheat and so I came back home and here I am, and now I'm thinking, God! Where did I go wrong?

Therapist: I'm incredibly impressed by that story. If I can just make sure I've understood. You were in a marriage, for whatever reasons you weren't happy with that. You decided when the children had grown up to take the step of ending the relationship. You moved away, physically and geographically and you then did what most people do when we separate, you had one or two other relationships. Some of them bite the dust, as they often do when we are recently separated. You then met somebody eventually, but unfortunately this actually turned out to be 19 months in biting the dust. (*Summarising*)

Susanne: Yes.

Therapist: You had some very unpleasant experiences and you had to get the police involved. Breathe a sigh of relief, move on, meet somebody new, go to his own country with, no doubt, high hopes and find yet again that you are disappointed! And all this, this is in the throes of dealing with the experience of having cancer diagnosed and treated, and finally finding that you are free of that. It's a hell of a lot to have happened to somebody in just three of four years, isn't it? What impresses me is your resilience. I know it's a tough story, but it's also one of resilience, isn't it? (*Reframing*)

Susanne: Yes it is, but it is also difficult to come to terms with because I think, is it all my fault, what did I do? I mean some days it all gets to me and I don't even know why I'm bothering with any of it, why don't I just stay in bed, or why don't I just go out and spend every penny I've got. Why am I bothering?

Therapist: Is that what those intrusive thoughts tell you?

Susanne: Yes, they just take me over.

Therapist: So, some of the time things are more or less OK, and at other times these negative thoughts just kind of take you over? (*Externalising*)

Exceptions and resources

Therapist: So what I was trying to just get clear in my own mind, was that actually you've been through a really big transition in the last three or four years. It is also apparent to me that, each time you find yourself in a difficult relationship you have taken the decision to end it. You ended the marriage, responsibly it seems because you waited until the children had grown. You also recognised early on that you had not chosen well with the other two men, and ended those as well. This seems to me like someone who, contrary to what you said earlier, actually does make decisions, even if they are difficult ones. I'm sure you know that not everyone has the courage to end poor relationships, even violent ones. (*Reframing Susanne's experience*). And despite all of this, you say that some aspects of your life have been 'fabulous' on paper at least. (*Identifying exceptions*)

Susanne: Well, yes.

Therapist: And in addition to that you have some of those real down days, as one would. You see my point is that I can get the sense of something of the gravity and the horror and the unpleasantness of it all – and it is quite natural that we will get up on days like that and think 'Oh, life's a bitch and what's the point?' (*Pacing, matching the client's experience*)

On the other hand I'm really interested in those things you said about those bright moments you have and the laughter that you have – how do you manage to do that? (*Linking exceptions to the client's actions to create a sense of agency*)

Susanne: I don't know. It's just I've always been like it and, I say, you know, me and my brother, we just (giggles)…

Therapist: So would you say…

Susanne: He's hysterical!

Therapist: So is there a you, like so many of us, there are two of you. There's the 'down' you and there's the 'up' you, it's a dual kind of thing. If we could switch into the 'up' you more on demand, that might be helpful. At the moment, the down you tends to get the upper hand sometimes.

Susanne: Yes, yes, a lot of the time.

Therapist: And yet there are times when it doesn't. How do you have that happen? How do you manage to access the 'up' you? What are the circumstances when you can kind of switch it on like that?

Susanne: Well, the company I'm in, perhaps, and that was one of the things in my marriage, my husband was so miserable most of the time, you couldn't be very amusing when he was around.

Therapist: So, company's important.

Susanne: Yes.

Therapist: You've mentioned your brother and that's obviously a source of inspiration and sparkle in your life.

Susanne: And work. I mean I laugh at work, I mean, we are all very busy and sometimes the laughter is what helps us through it.

Summary and task

Therapist: I'm impressed by the way you have managed to keep your sense of humour intact despite your difficulties you have been through. I've also noticed how you have been laughing more as we have been speaking, so I guess I'm starting to see the 'up' you, whereas it was the other you that came into the room a little while ago.

Susanne: That's probably so, but I'm talking to you, you see. The problem is when I'm alone.

Therapist: Yes, I understand that, and that is why we are talking, isn't it? You've also identified some times when, even alone, you have still managed to keep those intrusive thoughts at bay. I'm interested in how you do that. After all, if you are alone and you have a lighter moment, you must be doing that for yourself, because you are alone. So I'm really curious about how you do that.

Can I ask you, between now and the next time we meet, to look out for when those lighter moments occur, especially when you are alone, so next time we meet we can discuss them?

Commentary

As Susanne tells her story, the helper, a therapist in this case, is continually listening for evidence of resourcefulness and examples of successes to counter the essentially negative narrative that Susanne has come to accept as her 'truth'. The therapist begins by clarifying what it is that Susanne wants to tackle, and while consistently acknowledging that things have been difficult and never diminishing or contradicting her version of things, it also starts to paint an image of Susanne as a resourceful woman who has been making decisions about her life, even while she was going through difficult times.

I have reproduced this brief discussion – part of a longer session – to illustrate how some simple conversational techniques can influence the way the conversation goes. In this case, the therapist could have followed Susanne's lead and focused on the story which described her as a woman who was slightly confused, feeling guilty, liable to choose the men in her life unwisely and invaded by rumination. Instead, as we have seen, for the attentive listener, there is ample evidence to challenge this. The aim here is not to prove Susanne wrong, nor even to change her perspective. It is to show her that there may be other perspectives she has not considered, and which would provide a better platform from which to move forward in her life. SFBT does not aim to change people's lives, but to identify the resources with which they can do it themselves. As de Shazer and colleagues (1986) wrote 'Our aim is to start the solution process rather than stop the complaint pattern.'

The conversation is based on the key assumptions of SFBT outlined in Chapter 4, but before that we'll look at what makes helping and therapy successful.

CHAPTER 3

The Ingredients of Success

What makes for successful outcomes? Clearly knowing where we want to go is vital if we are to reach any destination by choice, and agreeing goals with the client is one of the cornerstones of SFBT. But before we get to the steps that are involved in this approach in particular it is worth understanding what contributes to successful therapy in general. It is widely accepted that there are up to four hundred different models under the heading of psychotherapy and counselling (Dryden and Feltham 1993; Tallman and Bohart 2001).

Bewildering though this is, outcome studies have for many years shown that different therapeutic approaches have more in common than separates them. They are all equally effective in achieving successful outcome. Outcome here means client satisfaction and achievement of targets.

Many studies have now shown that there are certain elements in any healing encounter that are common to all, and that these are more important than any theories or techniques supporting the various approaches. These ideas have been in circulation for over fifty years. An early pioneer of this view was Jerome Frank who, in his classic *Persuasion and Healing*, explicitly said, 'No one has shown convincingly that one therapeutic method is more effective than any other for the majority of psychological illnesses,' and 'the specific effects of particular healing methods may be overshadowed by therapeutically potent ingredients shared by all.' Michael Lambert in 1992 put the case even more comprehensively by describing the contributory factors and to what degree each of these factors influences success in therapy. Taking a clear look at what these aspects are and how they relate to the outcome is of critical value in working with clients or service users in any relationship deemed to be 'therapeutic'.[1]

---

1   For a fuller description of these factors and Michael Lambert's findings see Hubble, Duncan and Miller 2001.

These central and decisive factors can be grouped under four main headings: client events and extratherapeutic factors; relationships; placebo, hope and expectancy; and model and technique.

Client events and extratherapeutic factors: 40 per cent

These are factors such as supportive elements in the client's life; personal characteristics, resources and even chance events can influence the process of change by up to 40 per cent. Since these occur in our clients' lives outside the sessions they can really empower them by demonstrating self-sufficiency and reinforcing the dictum 'change happens anyway'. Examples might include such things as tenacity, religious belief, a sense of loyalty, past successes and even something that happened because they were 'in the right place at the right time'.

It is obvious that not all clients bring the same degree of motivation on entering the relationship. Equally, it can be seen that we are all, to varying degrees and with differing results, the product of our life experiences. Clients will begin the therapeutic process widely varying in those characteristics that might eventually contribute to success. Qualities like self-awareness, openness to change, cognitive style, ability to relate, self-esteem – not to mention the more immediate necessity of openness to the therapeutic enterprise – will all bring relative advantage or handicap to the process.

Another facet of the client's life over which the therapist has no control, but which can have a major influence on results, is their support structure. A supportive social network, especially marriage or an equivalent, stable relationship, is known to have a positive impact on physical and emotional health and recovery rates. From an SFBT perspective social support has potential, not simply because of the direct encouragement that may result but also due to the interactive nature of relationships. More 'positive' behaviour towards others is generally reciprocated in some way and this reinforces the process.

Finally, there is the question of 'chance' occurrences: a job offer, watching an inspiring movie, a long lost friend resurfacing or simply an unexplained 'good day'. Positive events in an individual's life bolster self-esteem, reinforce learning and confidence, and provide proof that we are 'on the right track' with our choices and decisions.

But what constitutes 'positive'? The inherent outlook of the person concerned and their manner of explaining events to themselves of course largely dictate this (Seligman 1995). People who (like many of our clients) have low self-esteem, for example, or who are depressed, or anxious, who have suffered a series of setbacks in life are inclined to have, at least temporarily, a pretty negative outlook, and are likely to view things with pessimism. And pessimists have a tendency to explain away positive events either as a fluke or attributable to something other than themselves.[2] Conversely they are often all too ready to take the blame for any negative events that occur. A key function of therapy is to help clients adopt a slightly more balanced view of life; taking credit for the good events and not accepting unreasonable or unproven responsibility for the bad. Helping clients identify aspects of their experience which challenge negative beliefs or interrupt debilitating patterns can start to give them a new perspective on their situation and provide an impetus for change.

Extratherapeutic aspects are 'unquestionably the most common and powerful of the common factors in therapy'. (Hubble *et al.* 2001). Understanding this means that we can harness a horse that is already going in the right direction. But, since the client will not have noticed or will have disregarded them, we'll have to look for, and help them recognise, the benefits inherent in these factors.

Relationship factors: 30 per cent

Although Lambert placed this second in order of importance, when asked in follow-up clients will often first say that some aspect of the relationship with the therapist was significant in them getting the results they wanted. Relationship factors contribute 30 per cent to the equation. They are more important than technique and include what is generally known as the core conditions of the therapeutic alliance – empathy, positive regard, warmth, congruence and genuineness – plus a range of other qualities such as sincere respect, trust, caring, support and encouragement. They also bring in client perceptions of the therapist's level of competence, confidence and honesty. Whether we are talking about therapy in its conventional sense, or social work, education, social rehabilitation or some other alliance, little can be achieved without first establishing what I refer to as a 'robust' working relationship.

---

2 A negative explanatory style is a key component in the thinking, not just of the depressed person, but also in those who are vulnerable to clinical depression in the face of negative life experiences. For a fuller explanation of explanatory styles and their consequences see Seligman 1995.

Who is to judge whether the relationship fulfills these criteria? Well, it is interesting to note that, according to research (Hubble *et al.* 2001) what matters most is what the client thinks, rather than some externally rated set of conditions. This is reflected in the stance taken by SFBT: if you want to know how things are going, ask the client. It is the client's impressions that are the true barometer of how things are going, and, since the therapeutic relationship seems generally to succeed or fail in the first few sessions (Bachelor and Horvarth 2001), progress needs to be checked from time to time, not assumed.

The therapist can actively take steps to build rapport, listen attentively, show empathy and demonstrate belief in the client. Such a stance is par for the course in any branch of therapy, and should be present – though often it is not – in any 'caring' relationship. SFBT has distinct advantages in this respect, since it recognises and accepts the client's reality. Finding out about the natural complexities of another individual's unique inner world, their thoughts, feelings and responses to life, requires sincere and focused curiosity, in itself is a great rapport builder. With such a line of enquiry the client naturally starts to feel understood, and the therapist is better informed. As important are the questions used to elicit such information (of which more later), since they actively promote reflection and learning in the client, and help to uncover strengths previously ignored. More traditional approaches tend to have theories about problems and behaviour, and to be mechanistic in applying the remedy; once the problem can be diagnosed, then it can be treated. This also runs the risk of harming the relationship by alienating the client from the therapist and leaving the latter unaware of the client's real views and feelings (Stack Sullivan 1970).

The therapy relationship itself can in fact represent a therapeutic intervention (Bachelor and Horvarth 2001), but despite the importance of these factors they do not very often get the attention they merit in training programmes. Perhaps that is because, whereas the other contributory aspects involve skills that can be relatively easily studied, it is harder, though not impossible, to pin down how to build and maintain relationships, much less teach it.[3] Nevertheless, the leading researchers in the field are calling for less 'medicalisation' of the therapeutic relationship and a greater emphasis on building and monitoring the

---

3   The skills can be broken down and taught, but just as with music where some people can learn the theory but never master an instrument well enough to be called a musician, so there are people who can understand the relationship theory and never be really comfortable relating to others.

interaction. Students should be provided with training, they say, not only in developing a strong alliance with their clients. They should also learn how to monitor it, and diagnose and repair problems that occur within the relationship. Bachelor and Horvarth sum up the true range and complexity of their subject by concluding: 'At its core, the therapeutic relationship remains an intensely human, personal and essentially unique encounter... every therapeutic engagement entails an (appointment) with the unknown and demands that the therapist remain open to the uniqueness of the client's world, ready to be surprised and moved at each meeting' (2001, p.163).

Placebo, hope and expectancy: 15 per cent

Placebo, hope and expectancy account for 15 per cent of improvement. The powerful role of these influences in people's lives is unquestionable; the clinical research literature, and the evidence of our daily lives, confirms this. The importance of expectancy has been known for thousands of years and yet, until very recently, has been largely disregarded when thinking about therapy. Expectancy relates to belief, on the part of both client and therapist, in the product or approach being used, the client's awareness that they are involved in a treatment process and the credibility of the professional with whom they are engaged.

The placebo response – where the patient or client improves because of their belief in the efficacy of treatment – has been demonstrated across such a wide range of problems and modes of treatment that it may be considered 'a true general ingredient in all clinical situations' (Rossi 1986). In medicine, from where the term placebo effect has been imported, it has come to be regarded more as a nuisance than a benefit. Its usefulness has been generally limited to double-blind drug trials. The theory here is that an active substance (the drug or procedure being tested) will outperform a placebo. The difference in results obtained between active and inert substances demonstrates the efficacy of the drug. The fact that a significant proportion of patients improved on pills containing nothing more than sugar or bread was regarded by all but a small minority of medical practitioners as non-scientific and therefore unreliable (Greenberg 2001). These 'non-specific' (i.e. psychological) treatment gains were rarely officially sanctioned for their therapeutic potential.[4] Nevertheless, and precisely because it has been so rigorously recorded in so many well-controlled studies, the healing potential of the placebo response is an established fact of life in all cultures.

The importance of hope (and the impact of hopelessness) should never be underestimated. 'Hope is the greatest gift we can offer our clients', say Berg and Dolan (2001, p.85). Assumptions about the future have a powerful effect on our present state and hope is an important facet of healing in both the developed and non-industrialised societies (Frank and Frank 1991). 'Hope comes about largely as a result of the patient's confidence and trust in a healer', says Lawrence Le Shan, the psychotherapist renowned for his work with cancer patients (Bolletino and Le Shan 1997, p.104). In his book *The Healing Heart* (1983), which has become the classic on the central role of faith, hope and optimism in healing, Norman Cousins describes how an atmosphere of genuine hopefulness, faith and confidence can enable the patient to optimise his or her prospects.

In SFBT these factors are used deliberately to empower the client, encourage optimism and facilitate change. It goes without saying that if the therapist cannot adopt an appropriate degree of expectancy and hope in themselves with regard to the client's prospects, they would be failing the client. It may help here to make a distinction: hope is definitely not the same thing as optimism. It is not conviction that something will turn out well, but the certainty that something makes sense, regardless of how it turns out. To quote Vaclav Havel, 'Hope is not prognostication. It is an orientation of the spirit, an orientation of the heart' (cited in Symynkywicz 1991, p.24).

Model and technique: 15 per cent

Despite the fact that professional training, theory and practice are increasingly oriented towards specific techniques and treatment approaches, and the vehemence with which people have always tended to promote or defend their models, there is no significant difference in outcome rates between the many and various approaches to therapy (Ogles, Anderson and Lunnen 2001, p.215). The choice of model,

---

4   Historically, however, the placebo effect has been used systematically in medicine, given that until the twentieth century most medicines given by doctors were medically inert. "The history of medical treatment until relatively recently is the history of the placebo effect" (Shapiro 1959, p.303)

therefore, cannot be a major contributor to positive outcome. Factors under this heading – which includes beliefs, techniques and procedures relating to the particular approach or model – account for 15 per cent of improvement in therapy. This also covers the perceived rationale of the approach and any 'technical' explanations for the client's difficulties.

This needs a little qualification on two points:

1. There are differences in the *duration* of therapy, depending on the model used, but Frank suggests that this is due to the beliefs of the therapist about how quickly they can obtain results more than anything else (Talmon 1990). And, whatever the duration, the greatest change still occurs 'in the early stages of treatment' (Snyder, Michael and Cheavens 2001, p.184), more precisely 'in 6–8 sessions' (Hubble, Duncan and Miller 1997)

2. Specific techniques are more effective than others for some distinct conditions (sexual difficulties, anxiety disorders and phobias for example), and in some circumstances the opposite may happen. For example, techniques that encourage introspection and analysis are less effective, and therefore contra-indicated, with depression (Seligman 1998).

To clarify what is meant by model and technique, a *model* is said to be a collection of beliefs or unifying theory about causes of complaints, and what is needed to bring about change for a given condition (Ogles *et al.* 2001). Models generally specify *techniques,* actions which are based on or comply with the logic of the model.

That a chosen model contributes so little to the final result may be troubling for those of us who have spent thousands of hours and a small fortune getting qualified in our chosen area. Naturally, many researchers have studied their specific approach to demonstrate its superiority over other forms of therapy. It is therefore all the more surprising that none has carried off the prize.

Clients don't care about technique
This does not mean that training, technique and theoretical approach are unnecessary or unimportant, simply that they are of more interest to the

therapist than the client. People seeking help with their difficulties don't generally care about the techniques we use, they simply want relief.[5] As professionals we all need a guiding philosophy, ethical foundation and professional boundaries for guidance. But we should not get carried away by our theories, because if we do we risk mistaking the recipe for the cake.

For anyone wishing to be more effective in their work an understanding of what makes for a successful outcome is obviously important. Why though, since this book obviously promotes SFBT, should I put such emphasis on factors which would seem to make interest in any one particular approach redundant? It is because the principal assumptions of SFBT, outlined in the next chapter, so reliably echo the common factors detailed here. While, as we have seen, none of these factors is unique to any approach, guiding ideas – such as seeing the client as resourceful, creating a collaborative relationship, harnessing expectation and recognising the importance of clients' beliefs – form the central ethos of SFBT rather than being peripheral to some other theory of operation.

---

5   I have said 'don't generally' because I know that a minority do in fact ask for a specific types of intervention, hypnosis for example.

CHAPTER 4

The Key Assumptions of SFBT

Practitioners of SFBT tend to avoid discussions about theories in favour of practical steps aimed at discovering how the client views his or her situation and how they interact with the world. In whatever setting the work is being done, clients are regarded as resourceful, and as experts on their own lives.

Rather than being seen as broken and dysfunctional, they are considered to be functioning and resourceful. Though they may well need help in some area of their lives this does not mean that they are useless or helpless. They may simply have lost touch with, or, for that matter, may never have recognised their existing qualities and potentials. SFBT seeks to identify and develop those resources, to reconnect the client with them and to encourage their participation in creating a more satisfying future for themselves. The strengths and abilities clients carry with them are the seeds from which solutions can be created.

There is no need for a theory when studying new terrain. Indeed, if we think of discussions with our clients as explorations, and theories as maps, it is easy to see how we might miss vital landmarks while looking at the map instead of really studying our client.

These are the main assumptions of SFBT:

- Clients have strengths and resources.
- The relationship between therapist and client has therapeutic value.
- Change happens all the time.
- A small change will generate larger change.
- Rapid change is possible.
- The focus is on the present and the future.
- Clear goals are essential.

- The attempted solution may be part of the problem.

- The focus is on people not problems.

- 'Resistance' is a function of the relationship.

- Knowing the cause of the problem is not necessary to do effective therapy.

Clients have strengths and resources

Clients have strengths and resources which can be brought to bear in resolving the complaint. In contrast to searching for the cause of the problem or identifying what the client is doing wrong – both of which amplify the negative aspects of the client's life – asking about the client's successes, skills and resources refocuses their attention on what is working in their lives. This not only starts to change the way they appraise themselves, it also determines the direction of therapy and empowers both the helper and the client.

We all have abilities and strengths that we overlook or take for granted. Some of these will be individual; an interest or hobby, or a challenge overcome. Others are more general, shared by many people, like a fondness for animals or a talent for gardening. It is a feature of SFBT to make use of any aspects of the client's environment which could be usefully employed to facilitate the process. Writing on this aspect of therapy – a development of the work of Milton Erickson – Jeffrey Zeig said: 'If it's part of the patient's life, it may be useful in achieving a therapeutic goal AND if the patient brings it, it's probably more potent than anything the therapist can introduce into the situation' (Zeig and Munion 1999, p.42).

The relationship between therapist and client has therapeutic value

As I outlined in the previous chapter, the relationship between client and therapist is of fundamental importance. A robust working relationship is essential to the process. By 'robust' I mean all the aspects such as respect, trust, warmth that have traditionally been the hallmarks of the therapeutic alliance. But I would add that honesty, curiosity and openness on the part of the therapist are just as important. The aim is that both participants should feel safe and confident enough to be able to express themselves naturally, freely and even with humour where the opportunity allows. As with any healthy relationship, this one must be able to resolve interpersonal difficulties, clear up misunderstanding and have space for the individuals to show themselves as they are, without relying on some façade. Robust, according to the thesaurus, also connotes being vigorous, healthy, hearty, full-bodied, strong and tough. If all this seems a little over the top for a relationship which must after all be conducted professionally, consider the words of Cas Schaap and colleagues writing on this topic: 'A constructive relationship between client and therapist seems therefore the condition "sine qua non" for therapeutic change. In order to increase the effectiveness of psychotherapy, these neglected mechanisms of change should be theoretically specified and systematically studied' (Schaap *et al.* 1993, p.7).

SFBT is an active process that requires curiosity, confidence and well-developed interpersonal skills on the part of the person in the role of therapist. How quickly such a relationship develops will of course vary from client to client, as will the degree to which the qualities above are achieved. As the likely outcome of our activities is determined within the first few sessions, this is the foundation on which all our future efforts are built.

Change happens all the time

There is a Hindustani expression, 'The clock strikes differently every hour.' Even the things which appear most constant are perpetually in flux: change is happening all the time. We often expect constancy in our lives and yet nothing is actually as stable and unchanging as we pretend. Whether we are talking about our mood, the climate, the balance of political power, our enjoyment of a particular pastime or any other aspect of life, the norm is variation and change, not the stability we imagine. Once we have understood this, we can start to look out for it and encourage the client to do the same. The aim of therapy is to bring about change, but if we are alert only for the change that we attribute to our therapeutic efforts we will miss huge opportunities to demonstrate to the client that change is not only possible, but inevitable. Change is happening anyway, and it is much easier to help something along that is already moving, to accelerate or amplify the process, than it is to persuade a static object to move.

SFBT majors on this phenomenon of the inevitability of change by seeking to identify and amplify it, by noticing when change occurs spontaneously and how further change can be promoted. This starts by asking about any positive changes the client may have noticed before the first session (pre-session change), continues during the session in enquiries about unexpected changes the client may or may not have noticed (exceptions, problem-free times) and follows on after the session by suggesting the client look out for positive changes that might occur over the coming week (or until the next session).

This encourages a shift in the client's thinking habits and their perceptions in relation to their difficulties, which will impact on their sense of control, self-esteem and motivation (Hewstone 1989).

A small change will generate larger change

Since change is happening anyway, a nudge in the right direction may be all that is needed. Even in situations where a good deal of support may be necessary because of the predicament a particular client is in, as long as we focus on small steps they are frequently able to manage alone if we can 'start the ball rolling'. Once something, however small, in their situation changes it will trigger other minor changes. This in turn leads to other, more significant developments, and so on. It is not only difficulties that are self-perpetuating. Just as noticing something we don't like about ourselves or our situation can start to act like a self-fulfilling prophecy, increasing our pessimism and our conviction that we have a problem, so noticing positive change can start a virtuous cycle of improvement; as we start feeling a little more optimistic it leads to the confidence to attempt further changes. The therapist's role becomes increasingly 'hands off' as the process gathers momentum, until finally we are redundant.

Aiming for small changes also minimises the risk of discouraging setbacks for the client early in the process. By deliberately scaling down goals to be certain that they are within achievable limits, and designing tasks that fall comfortably within the client's range of abilities (though not necessarily within their previous experience), the therapist helps ensure success. Better a small success than a large failure. Writing on this topic Michael Hoyt and Robert Rosenbaum say 'In every stage, it is better to move with a small step or give a very small task that the therapist is confident that the patient is ready to carry out than a big task that might evoke fear and ambivalence' (Talmon 1990, p.17).

Aiming for small changes does not mean having low expectations. Taking things slowly and carefully is perfectly compatible with having high hopes for our clients. In fact it makes success more likely and durable for several reasons: small changes are likely to be easier to assimilate and require less adjustment on the part of the client; where clients may be unsure of making changes small ones might even go unnoticed and therefore less easily opposed; little differences as they occur can generate hope and expectation of more change thus facilitating the process; and it will be easier for some clients to take credit for little things because it seems plausible.

At all times progress will be dictated by the client's willingness and abilities, so setting our sights low to ensure success will in no way limit them; if they want to move faster or further than we have suggested, they will.

Rapid change is possible

Change can happen quickly, no matter how long-standing the problem. There is no link between the length of time a client has been struggling with their difficulties and the time needed to start the process of change (Watzlawick, Weakland and Fisch 1974). We seem to believe, often, in a sort of natural law which says that if a problem has been around for a long time, it will take a long time to fix. But there is no proof of this except our own beliefs. If we can free ourselves from this self-limiting idea, rapid change is possible. In fact, if we look in the right places we usually find it has been happening already, but has simply gone unnoticed. This is not to say that all situations respond equally quickly, but even those that need a little more time than the average three to six sessions usually demonstrate some positive change early in the process.

This does not mean that we make light of the client's very real difficulties or ignore that they may be hopelessly resigned to 'more of the same'. We simply do not buy into it. There is after all, another side to every coin, even if the coin has been in circulation a long time. And looking at the other side of the coin means doing something different from that which the client has typically done when thinking about or reacting to their problem. 'Once we begin to look for differences instead of similarities, it is practically impossible... not to get new ideas. For the habit of asking 'How do these things differ?' or 'How might this be different?' is one of the basic techniques of originality or creativeness' (Johnson 1946, p.28).

So, long-standing problems are seen not as chronic symptoms indicating some deep, underlying defect in the individual, but as the result of the repeated mishandling of a difficulty. The way the client has been approaching the problem or behaving in a given situation, far from helping, may actually be maintaining the problem. When we approach the difficulty from a new perspective, one which involves fresh thinking about how people get stuck with their difficulties, the longevity of the problem bears no relation to its permanence and a ten-year-long problem can be addressed with just as much optimism as a difficulty that surfaced a month ago (Watzlawick and Weakland 1977).

The focus is on the present and the future

In the introduction to an influential book about the nature of change Milton Erickson wrote 'Psychotherapy is sought not primarily for enlightenment about the unchangeable past but because of dissatisfaction with the present and a desire to better the future' (Watzlawick *et al.* 1974, p.ix). SFBT focuses on where the client wants to go rather than where they have come from, on what they want to have happen from now on rather than what has happened to them, on how things will be rather than how they were. This does not mean that the past is taboo. Clients will often want to speak about the past and it would be churlish and insensitive to refuse them the opportunity. This can also yield constructive information and since we are all the products of our experience, the past of course provides rich data about us. When solution focused we are tuned in to listen to stories of the client's past, not for chronicles of failure and disadvantage, but for examples of resilience and success (Berg and Dolan 2001).

Since the cause of the problem, if there is one, always resides in the past, there is little we can do to change it in the present. It is true that some clients like to know about the cause of a problem, but this will be incidental to improvement in their situation, not indispensable to it. Transformation is concerned with *what* happens, not *why* it happens (Watzlawick *et al.* 1974). Most would agree that we are not working to influence the cause, we are seeking to deal with its effect, the impact on the client's life in the here and now.

Clear goals are essential

SFBT starts by eliciting clear goals for the intervention. Since solution focused therapists accept that every client is different there is no notion of standard 'fixes' for standard problems. There are many valid ways of living one's life, and only the client can know what their goals might be. They may need help in deciding the focus, or where they want to start in the case of multiple goals, but the decision about what to work towards is always theirs. They may also need guidance to ensure that they do not aim for goals which are unrealistic, and support until they feel confident enough to participate fully in attaining their goals. In the terminology of the approach goals are 'negotiated' with the client, to make sure that they fit the right criteria (realistic, achievable etc., see the section on goal-setting on pp.126–128). One of the golden rules in deciding on goals is to keep them small, at least at the outset. This will help build confidence in the process as well as reducing the likelihood of a setback due to failure. Goals can be reviewed and modified as therapy progresses, though this is often not necessary. As we have seen, some clients may only need help in taking the first, small steps and can continue the process by themselves from there on.

The attempted solution may be part of the problem

There is a saying: 'If you always do what you always did you'll always get what you always got.' Without realising it, when attempting to solve a problem we frequently 'do more of the same' even though our chosen strategy is not working. This leads to the phenomenon of 'the attempted solution becoming part of the problem' (Watzlawick *et al.* 1974).

> Maggie had a panic attack while doing the shopping, and so she started to avoid situations, like going into shops, which she believed might trigger another attack. A perfectly reasonable response, and one which seemed to work. Only now the problem is, she can't get her shopping done very easily because her avoiding tactics mean that she can't go into shops. No problem, by relying on her husband, John, and friends she manages to arrange her life so she need not run the risk of more attacks. She still goes out every day to visit her ageing mother who lives a few streets away, but this is a familiar routine that Maggie manages well. If really pushed, she can just about manage to enter a shop by sticking close to John, but only if it is a shop she knows and one that is not too crowded.

The original problem, fear of having another panic attack, is now replaced by the practical limitations of her attempted solution. The problem now becomes that she cannot move around as she would like. She is doing nothing about the original difficulty (panic attacks) and is now involved in creating a new problem for herself (can't go to shops). As long as Maggie continues with her attempts to solve the problem of panic attacks by avoiding the situations she blames as the cause, she is unlikely to extricate herself from this self-reinforcing cycle.

This is not limited to the client's own strategies, we see the same patterns wherever repeated attempts fail to solve a problem. Take for example a fairly common scenario between teenagers and their parents, say, asking them to be home by a certain time. It is virtually guaranteed that a situation will arise where the child gets home later than the deadline. The typical parental response to this apparent flouting of their authority is to impose another deadline or more limiting rules, say, grounding the child. In response to this 'solution' the child is likely to become ever more creative in his or her attempts at maintaining independence, thus increasing the alienation between parent and child and reducing still further the parent's fragile sense of authority over their offspring. How to most parents respond? By imposing still more rules…and so the situation escalates. God forbid that the family falls into the hands of a misguided therapist whose well-meaning attempts simply continue with…more of the same!

The focus is on people not problems

Problems are a result of how the client is interacting with the world rather than existing in isolation as treatable entities. While there are common factors among people who are, for example, depressed, no two people experience the constellation of symptoms known as depression in the same way. Neither do they respond to them in the same way. Each client is unique and therefore each person's response to a set of circumstances will be unique to that individual. The traditional, and convenient, habit of grouping patients with the same sets of symptoms under headings often obscures this. People are not their labels and how each person reports their individual case of depression, drug dependency or insomnia will be entirely different and specific to them. A diagnostic label, if the client already has one, may be fine as a starting point for discussions. It will be harmful if we start treating the diagnosis rather than the person.

To avoid this, solution focused conversations swiftly turn to what the sufferer's symptoms mean for them and how they will be functioning when their difficulties are resolved or diminished.

SFBT views symptoms as problematic only if the patient says they are. Thus, the 'presenting complaint' may not be the same as the issue they want to work on. For example, someone with a drink problem may say that it is more urgent, for them, to deal with arguments with their partner than it is to reduce their drinking. When a third party or outside agency gets involved the process can get even more confusing. I was asked to see a teenager because, his mother said, he was being bullied. His description of the problem was quite different; he framed the 'bullying' as 'teasing', adding 'We all have to put up with that, if you don't react to it it's not a problem.' What was a problem for him was the disruptive behaviour of other pupils in class which was distracting him from his studies. So we worked on ways he could stay more focused and improve his results. How different it would have been if I had simply gone with the label of bullying without first checking with the client.

Recognising and accepting the client's reality is a vital first step. Understanding, as far as we can, how they experience their situation and letting them know it also builds rapport and encourages their autonomy at the same time. We are also more effective and efficient when we work with the client's belief system (Berg and Dolan 2001), rather than attempting to re-educate them into a way of thinking that may suit us, or the society they live in, but which does not fit with what they want.

'Resistance' is a function of the relationship

SFBT sees resistance or hostility as a function of the relationship rather than a permanent attribute or disposition of the client. It is assumed that everyone has the ability to change and that under the right circumstances – for them – they will be willing and able to. Therefore, if they do not appear to want do so at this precise moment in time it is up to the therapist to do something different (Haley 1976), rather than expecting the client to change their attitude.

We all come across situations where the person we are working with appears to be dragging their feet. They may say they are willing to work towards goals but when they return to subsequent sessions it is obvious that they have taken no action to match their words. Or worse, they simply don't engage in the discussions we are attempting to have with them.

Part of the problem here is that our training for working with clients, patients or service users, has prepared us for doing it with people who are candidates for change. In real life, however, we come across those who appear recalcitrant, unwilling to engage with us as 'good clients' should. We are unprepared for this and generally feel underskilled. Faced with such testing situations it is very reassuring for the therapist to identify the client as 'resistant'; to be unready or unwilling to change because of something that is wrong with them.

Solution focused thinking sees this scenario from a different angle. It does not identify hostility or resistance in the client as an obstacle, it recognises it as information about the client's beliefs, feelings and, consequently, their level of motivation to engage. Rather than attempting to compel participation by applying pressure or trying to coerce the client in some way – which would be doing more of the same when something is not working – this approach asks the therapist to look to themselves and their understanding of the client's predicament. The question here then is 'What have I missed?' We start by asking it of ourselves and may even ask the client.

In my workshops I illustrate the subject of the client's apparent unwillingness to change with two questions: 'Has anyone ever tried to change you?' and 'Did it work?' Most people, when faced with a perceived demand that they change, react by digging their heels in. When we do change it is generally in the context of a relationship marked by respect, trust, goodwill or love. If ever we comply with a request to alter ourselves or our behaviour because of threats, persuasiveness, manipulation or simply to please the other person, it is likely to be, at best, unwilling and short lived.

Thinking about clients in this way is a salutary reminder to those of us who work with people – whether our role is as therapist, probation officer, social worker, teacher or one of numerous others – that the onus for engaging them relies on us making it relevant and appropriate to their needs and wishes. In other words, that it is up to us to find a way of engaging them. This may seem an onerous duty, particularly in some settings where so-called 'clients' are told to attend, in effect ordered to see us, and therefore could not reasonably be expected to engage. Once we get used to the idea, however, it opens the way to working genuinely collaboratively with our clients. This is usually less tiring and more productive, opening the way to more efficient therapy.

Knowing the cause of the problem is not necessary to do effective therapy

Since we are concerned about consequences, rather than causes, it is not necessary to understand the reason the client has their problem. This flies in the face of conventional thinking on problem-solving, nevertheless it is so (De Bono 1994; O'Hanlon and Weiner Davis 1989). Consistent with the view that there is no direct link between cause and effect, viewing problems simply as a 'the unpredictable events of living' (Lipchik 2002), means switching from an introspective search for the root of the difficulty to a more active quest for ways to deal with the impact of those events, whatever they may have been.

Clients, of course, frequently ask 'Why?' In my own practice I have found that about a third of those I see want to understand the reason for their complaint. Following the solution focused principle of using whatever the client brings into the room, I use this as an opportunity to turn the question on its head with another one: 'Which is most important to you, to know that the problem goes away or to know why it has gone?'[1] In most cases this elicits the response that it is more important to be free of the problem. When people really do want to know the 'why' of things they tell me, and we'll explore it and spend some time speculating on *possible* causes. I always take care to separate this discussion about explanations from efforts to resolve or ease the client's difficulties; these are completely separate issues and they should not be mixed up. As Eve Lipchik says 'Cause and effect thinking is a road no solution-focused therapist should travel' (2002, p.19).

In summary, since we are respectful of the client's needs, if they wish to understand more about possible causes of their difficulties we should not deny them the opportunity for a little explanation. But it should be made clear that searching for cause and dealing with effect are separate exercises and, as soon as we reasonably can, we should draw the conversation back to where the exercise is intended to go; towards identifying the client's skills...for solutions. The other course may, unwittingly, lengthen or complicate therapy. If the client already believes that they know the cause of their problems, it will have to be judged on its merits and potential disadvantages. If it is not limiting or harming them there is probably no need to challenge it.

---

1   Apart from checking how much the client really needs to know the cause, this question does a couple of other things. It is a double bind. A double bind creates an illusion of alternatives so the client can't answer without accepting the possibility of change, it also presupposes success, since in either case the problem will go.

Ask the client

The therapist's stance can be guided by the main assumptions given in this chapter reinforced by the ability to listen effectively, observe astutely and think creatively. Repeated studies have shown that most people in therapy stay in treatment for a very short time, many for just a single session, having got what they need at that time from the initial meeting. The average number of sessions across all the different approaches is three to six (Talmon 1990). In view of this, and the points covered in Chapter 3 on the common factors, we need to make every minute of every session count by actively doing our best to make a difference. The guiding principles of SFBT make it possible to be effective by ensuring a stance which builds on the naturally occurring phenomena of the process and constructively engaging the client's talents as we go along. It does not mean, by the way, neglecting the important aspects of any human relationship such as care and concern for the client's need to be heard and supported, regard for their feelings and true respect for their perceptions about themselves, including any fears or uncertainties which might temporarily be holding them back.

Therapy is about change and while the focus of attention is on enabling the desired adjustments in the client's perceptions and responses, we should not neglect the necessity to change what *we* do in response to the verbal and non-verbal feedback from the client. Getting 'stuck' is often the result of ignoring information on how they think or feel about some aspect of what we are attempting to do with them. We therefore need to cultivate in ourselves the ability to be able to observe our own beliefs, motivations and ambitions for the client so as to ensure that what we think matches what they want. In the final analysis there is really only one way to know this, so, as the saying goes, 'If in doubt, ask the client.'

CHAPTER 5

The Building Blocks of SFBT

We construct our reality

Primo Levi, a chemist by training, was interned at Auschwitz during the Second World War, a period for which he said he would never have expected to feel any nostalgia. In his collection of essays entitled *Other People's Trades* he notes with surprise the 'singular power of the mind' to let happy memories survive and to slowly stifle the others.

> I have recently seen again an old fellow prisoner and we had the usual conversations of veterans: our wives noticed and pointed out to us that in two hours of conversation we had not brought up even a single painful memory, but only the rare moments of remission or the bizarre episodes. (Levi 1990, p.106)

In his case he apparently attributes this to a natural filtering process. Whether it is as conveniently automatic as this is a debatable point, since quite obviously not everyone benefits from such protection. What it illustrates to me, however, is the ability we have to construct our reality. What we choose to recall and focus on shapes how we think and feel.

While nobody would deny the horror and revulsion of the events Levi obliquely referred to, there can be no benefit, over fifty years later, in reliving the horror of them. So it is when we are having conversations with our clients. We can choose what to discuss. When we can seek out the 'rare moments of remission', as Levi puts it, we help our clients construct a more empowering frame of reference as a starting point to the rest of their lives. We are not denying their past, we are simply not reconstructing it for them.

Focusing on the positive aspects of our experiences has suffered in the past from misunderstandings about what has been referred to as 'positive thinking', with its evocations of rose tinted glasses and silver linings. Research in psychology over the past decade, however, has vindicated the positive thinkers; we now know that focusing on strengths and the more optimistic aspects of our experience not only produces healthier and more resilient individuals, it actually leads to a snowballing effect so that people's satisfaction with their lives improves. Martin Seligman's work under the banner of positive psychology[1] demonstrates that:

> Experiences that induce positive emotion cause negative emotion to dissipate rapidly. [Our] strengths and virtues…function to buffer against misfortune and against psychological disorders, and they may be the key to building resilience. The best therapists do not merely heal damage; they help people identify and build their strengths and their virtues. (Seligman 2003, p.xiii)

Positive psychology is now a recognised branch of the discipline with a continually growing body of scientific research to support its claims.[2]

Helping people to develop greater resilience is a strategy that should be used by all competent psychotherapists. Seligman calls these buffering strengths and they include interpersonal skills, self-awareness, optimism, courage, honesty, perseverance, realism, capacity for pleasure, putting troubles into perspective, future mindedness and finding purpose.

Strengths not problems

Identifying strengths and positive traits, SFBT practitioners would rightly say, is what they have been doing for years. One of the most important aspects of positive psychology is that it has resulted from the efforts of a group of researchers who are coming from an entirely different direction. Their work gives credence to the stance taken by SFBT precisely because they are not part of the same tradition. It is demonstrating that the phenomenon described by Primo Levi, though not as inevitable as he seems to imply, really can happen when it gets a little help.

---

1   I am referring to Seligman's work because, in controlled studies, it has demonstrated, and continues to demonstrate, the benefits of focusing on the positive. The field of positive psychology involves studying a far wider range of the aspects of human experience and the social institutions that contribute to a sense of well-being and fulfilment than those I have referred to, and it is quite separate from SFBT.

2   The American Psychological Association has a website devoted to the subject at www.positivepsychology.org.apaintro.htm.

We now come to some ideas of how to structure a discussion with the client or service user.[3] The aim is to create a focus led by their goals or aspirations. The therapist, working in a collaborative role, acts as guide or facilitator to ensure that the process remains on track. Focusing on strengths, differences and exceptions rather the problems or pathology begins to open up possibilities for the client.

The key difference compared with other support roles is that the stance of the SFBT therapist is one curiosity and ingenuousness meeting the client's expert knowledge of their life (known as taking a one-down position in the solution focused vocabulary), rather than the reverse which has traditionally been the model. This means putting aside our interpretations and assumptions and filling in the gaps in our understanding *only* with information supplied by the client.

To illustrate this, think about the more conventional 'healer–patient' relationship for a moment. It places the therapist as the expert who has the knowledge – holds the keys – that will unlock the doors to the complex world of symptoms, causes and treatments for the patient's ailment. The implication is that the healer knows what is best for their patient. The patient is in a one-down position in relation to this expertise and must defer to superior knowledge without ever developing a full understanding of the rationale behind their treatment (Balint and Balint 1961; Stack Sullivan 1970).

The solution focused approach reverses this situation; the therapist of course has expert knowledge of his or her field, but not of the client's life. We will be able to draw on our skills and understanding in acting professionally, ethically and even using specific techniques to facilitate the process (active listening, empathising, skilful questioning, tasking, etc.). For professional purposes, and among colleagues, we may even use the jargon of our profession (dysfunction, personality disorder, disruptive behaviour, etc.). In conversations with our client, however, when speaking about *them*, *their* lives and how *they* go about *their* business, we are not experts. In short, we are ignorant about what makes them who they are. The only way we can begin to understand anything of their experiences, values, motives, wishes and ambitions is by asking them. So we build an understanding based on *their* expert knowledge. This will mean drawing out information that the client will often have overlooked about themselves

---

3   For convenience I refer to the client in the singular throughout this section. The 'client' may also be a group, a couple or a whole family.

and their experience. It also means that we have to cultivate the habit in ourselves of focusing entirely on the client for the information we need rather than listening to our theories, our assumptions and our predictions, however well founded they are in training or professional expertise.

In attending to strengths rather than pathology, establishing a clear direction or focus for the intervention, and co-constructing with the client a way forward, we work towards solutions in the form of improved outcomes in the client's interactions with life.

The steps outlined below describe how to go about it. They are clear and concise in order to communicate the ideas, but this also presents a dilemma. One of the common comments about SFBT is that it is formulaic and mechanistic, precisely because the instructions can be presented in a step-by-step way. Naturally, I do not agree with this criticism, but I can see how it arises. To use the analogy of a recipe for cooking a cake, we do not complain about the way the list of ingredients and instructions, or rules, for using them are presented (unless our cake is a failure), and we accept that successful baking requires a range of skills which, though they are not captured in the instructions for baking the cake, are nevertheless a necessary part of good baking. These supplementary skills – the art of cooking if you like – may be explained in a different part of the cookery book, but they are not included in the recipe.

Paul Watzlawick (1978), writing on the 'rules' involved in speaking the client's language, said that the relevant chapters he had devoted to the topic: 'are designed to promote the *understanding* of rules; their *application* must necessarily be left to the skills, the inventiveness and presence of mind of the therapist, and to the unique circumstances of every given situation' (p.49, his emphasis).

The rest of this chapter is concerned with the main ingredients of a solution focused interaction.

1. Establish a safe working relationship

As we have seen, the quality of the therapeutic relationship is of fundamental importance. Great things are possible when the client perceives that he or she is in a sincere, honest and supportive alliance. Conversely, a lot of time and effort will be wasted if this is not the case.

Of course, a productive relationship can take many forms. Clients present themselves in a wide variety of different ways. While some are naturally caring and sharing, others can be challenging and competitive;

logical and analytical; cautious and mistrustful; cynical and sarcastic; or flippant and humorous. We are all as varied as human nature allows. No two clients will be the same and so no two therapeutic relationships will be. The therapist's job is to match his or her style, within reason, to that of the client, not the other way round (Chaika 2000). We all do this unconsciously to some extent anyway as part of our natural set of interpersonal skills. Therapists simply need to develop these innate abilities consciously to maximise trust and rapport. It also encourages cooperation and helps the client feel accepted and to speak more openly (Battino and South 1999).

As any relationship develops over time I am not suggesting that things must instantly 'gel', but one of the many advantages of SFBT is that it specifically directs the therapist towards behaviours that favour rapport building. The way we listen and the questions we ask are a good start. An attitude of enquiring curiosity not only helps the therapist to convey helpful interest, it tells the client that they are central to the discussion and sets the scene for working collaboratively. As a by-product, when we are truly and actively focused on the client's world it helps us to avoid our own interpretations, assumptions and attempts to 'diagnose' their difficulties (Haley 1976).

2. Help define a clear, specific focus for intervention

In any interaction it is useful to have some idea of the purpose and eventual outcome we are aiming for. Giving the session direction by learning what it is that the client wants to change will greatly enhance the process for both participants and setting goals is an essential part of the SFBT process. These are generally agreed in the first session, but, as being too goal focused could unwittingly appear to invalidate some of what the client has to say it should take second place to getting a clear idea of who the client is and what, in a more general sense, they would like to achieve. They will certainly have a story of some sort to tell, and this in itself will yield useful details and illustrations of resourcefulness, successes and exceptions. For example, even the most tragic and problem-laden tale will contain examples of persistence, courage or other virtues which can be picked up and developed by the therapist. So deferring the actual process of setting goals a little brings with it the advantages of showing due sensitivity to the client's needs and enabling the therapist to glean a better understanding of their situation.

Clients are seeking change in something that is spoiling the quality of their lives and so it is they who should define their goals, in discussion with the therapist, rather than the other way round. It is the therapist's job to ensure that these are achievable, realistic and fulfill the other criteria for a well-formed goal (see pp.126–128). Whether we actually use the term 'goals' – which may seem a little formal and intimidating to some clients – or choose instead to talk about 'aims of the session(s)', 'target', 'outcome' or some other description, we must ensure that they match these criteria.

Some agencies talk about 'goals' when really they mean that they want the client to do something or behave in a way that fits *their* objectives, not those of the client. A school might have the aim of reducing a student's disruptive behaviour in class, a prison might have the goal of reducing drug use among inmates. These will only qualify as goals when the client, in these cases the student or the prisoner, have participated in the development of the goals and agreed them. Attempts to impose goals, however desired and wholesome they may seem, are not only likely to fail, they will also discredit the process and drive a wedge between the therapist and their client.

3. Look for client resources

SFBT sees clients as resourceful and functioning, at least in some areas of their lives, however hopelessly they might view their situation. Even clients in the most challenging or frightening circumstances have resources that they probably will not have noticed. These may be particular skills or abilities they possess, people they know, experiences they have had or obstacles they have surmounted.

Living brings with it a whole range of factors and functions that can be drawn on to help balance a negative or problem dominated view of the world. Even if the only recognisably skilful thing the client has done all week is to turn up for their appointment on time, it demonstrates some strengths, however tenuous they appear in the face of the presenting problems. It is empowering to see oneself as a resourceful individual.

In contrast to this is easy for patients and clients to accept the belief that, because they are seeking the help of a professional, they automatically relinquish part of their identity as a functioning human being. Seeking help is not the same as being helpless. This is sometimes difficult to remember for the person in the role of helper or therapist. Our own views on who we are and what our job means can lead us to buy into the 'helpless client' type of thinking which will only diminish and disempower them further. It takes a deliberate act of will to step outside this conventional view and to look at the client as someone who has managed so far in their life and will probably continue to do so, with or without us.

Of course, when people are frightened or suffering they frequently do express themselves in hopeless and alarming terms and the last thing they need is someone denying or playing down how they see their situation. Recognition of the client's resourcefulness does not mean ignoring their pain and distress, it means viewing the suffering as part of their experience rather than as a definition of who they are.

4. Be curious about exceptions to the problem

No problem happens all the time and so there are always exceptions to the problem (Berg and Dolan 2001). Seeking them out will create hope by showing that the problem does not always exist or, at least, that there are times when it is less dominant. In the case of clients who are unable to discern any exceptions, we can then enquire how they manage so well despite the problem.

Exceptions to the problem come in many guises. Steve de Shazer and his team at the Brief Family Therapy Center refer to 'solution-talk' to describe the process of looking for exceptions, resources and recent changes in the client's life (as opposed to 'problem talk') (de Shazer 1994).

The therapist should enquire about problem-free times in detail, and as early as reasonable and possible in the session. Studies have shown that the sooner solution-talk is introduced into the discussions the earlier change happens and the shorter therapy will be (Lipchik 2002). All conversations, and therapeutic ones in particular, consist of far more than simply the outwardly visible interaction between the participants. As we speak, we are also engaged in intricate mental processes of assessing and reviewing what is going on, of interpreting and adjusting our ideas and responses in consequence. This process (greatly oversimplified here) happens consciously and also outside our conscious awareness. In answering our questions the client will have to mentally hunt around for information, and in so doing will not only unearth the details we are asking for, they will also begin to mobilise unconscious resources which can then be used in the construction of a plan of action (Zeig and Munion 1999). As a corollary, we should always remember that this process can be making far-reaching changes to the client's inner world not just during the therapy sessions, but also between and beyond our discussions with them (Talmon 1990).

This mental search is also beneficial because, if we are genuinely curious and probing about exceptions and changes, it will start to interrupt the client's routine patterns of response; it requires them to move outside their habitual and practised mental circuit. This is specially important with clients who have previously spent many months or even years 'in the system', where their practised responses have become almost automatic. Simply doing more of the same by repeating the questions that they have become used to answering serves no useful purpose (and can result in them becoming even more 'stuck'). Finding out how and when they have managed despite the problem, understanding the strategies for coping and identifying times when they are problem-free does something different, and helps them develop a more resourceful outlook.

People are usually more focused on the times in their lives when things go wrong than when they don't. Enquiring about exceptions quite often produces a visible change in the client's body posture or facial expression as new realisations about their situation begin to occur to them. Some say they are feeling a little better about themselves or at least a little less hopeless. Solution focused questions also encourage less constraining thinking habits when dealing with the inevitable future difficulties (that are part of life). Starting to balance the 'bad' with the 'good' in this way makes the most of the client's resources and enhances their self-esteem (Berg and Miller 1992).

5. Scale the situation now

The question 'On a scale of one to ten where are you now?', used creatively, helps to provide focus and to review progress later. It also provides a language for discussing ways in which the client may move forward; for example, by asking what it would take to nudge them one or two points up the scale (see Scaling in Chapter 7). Scaling helps move the conversation from the general to the specific and encourages the client to think incrementally about his or her difficulties and the way forward. Berg and Dolan (2001, p. 9) say 'We think of it as an anchoring tool that allows clients to measure, assess and evaluate their own situations.' It also provides a useful reference point for progress in later sessions.

The value of scaling, in my view, is often underestimated. We can forget that when a client is involved in answering scaling questions they are already doing therapy for themselves. They may not consciously register it at the time, but the realisation that there is something between 'all' and 'nothing' can be a revelation with a powerful effect. It also overcomes a common stumbling block that we can all identify with; with some tasks it is difficult to know how to make a start because they seem either too vague or too big. Questions like, 'What would it take to get you one point up on the scale?' or 'How will you know when you have reached five?' ask the client to focus on small steps and elicit information that can start to make their situation seem more manageable.

Scaling teaches a new and useful thinking skill to clients and, by definition, it presupposes change and movement. It also seems to 'fit' with the way many people think, most take to it readily.

6. Identify the client's level of motivation

The client's level of motivation is clearly critical and the therapist must find ways of involving and engaging them. Evidently, the client must feel that the process of therapy is appropriate to them. With clients who are willing participants in the process this does not present any difficulty (though their willingness should never be assumed, always check). Things get more difficult with clients who are hostile to the process, for example, when they have been told to attend therapy against their wishes, or when they think that the therapist is pushing for a goal that they do not share.

SFBT sees resistance as a function of the relationship, rather than a trait in the client's personality. It is easier to improve a relationship than it is to change someone's character. Reading uncooperative or resistant behaviour as information about how the client feels about the process (rather than blaming the client and giving up), the therapist responds by altering his or her behaviour so that the interaction becomes more fruitful (Schaap *et al.* 1993).

Our training rarely prepares us for working with uncooperative clients. Rather than turning the exercise into a struggle or a trial of wills it is more productive to ask ourselves questions like 'What have I missed?' or 'What will help this client accept or engage with me?' Viewing from this angle also reminds the therapist to focus on where the client wants to go, just in case it might have been forgotten. Another way of viewing the problem is to see the client not as unmotivated, but as motivated by something different from the declared aims of the therapy. In this case we need to align the therapy with their motivations in order to make increased cooperation possible. (See also the discussion of customers, complainants or visitors in Chapter 10.)

The skills involved in engaging clients (or the deficits when we fail to) do not belong to any school of therapy. They are part of the interpersonal skills common to all of us.[4] I mention this because in my workshops I often meet people who, because of their line of work, regularly have to deal with recalcitrant clients. In such cases it is easy to attribute 'failure' to the approach – in this case SFBT – when really it is a result of the interaction between the people involved. This in turn may be due to the unrealistic expectations of some outside agency or employer.[5]

Even in extreme cases, where the aims of the 'client' may seem to be at odds with those of the intervention, cooperation is possible. Child protection is such an example. Social workers and other child protection professionals quite clearly are not in an equal and balanced relationship with their service users, since they have legal and statutory powers over them. In their book *Signs of Safety* Turnell and Edwards say 'Surprising as it may seem, we firmly believe that a cooperative relationship is attainable between worker and family even when statutory intervention occurs and/or where other forms of coercion are used' (1999, p.35).

We hope that most of the clients we work with are motivated and wish to engage with us. In the cases where they are not, it is useful to invoke a solution focused approach to thinking about our own practice. Whatever line of work we are in, therapy, education, social work or

---

4   Though they are common to all but a very few people (those suffering from autism for example), we quite obviously do not all possess them to the same degree. Nevertheless, the social and interpersonal skills needed to build productive relationships belong in the domain of human interactions rather than being specific to any therapeutic approach. Furthermore, they can and should be learned by therapists. See Battino and South 1999; Hubble *et al.* 2001.

5   For example, I once met a group of prison drugs staff whose job it was to persuade prisoners into new habits. It is the goal of the system to stop people using drugs. While some prisoners undoubtedly will share this goal, others are unwilling to buy into it. Furthermore, the prisoners who agree to the goal do not do so because of the therapeutic approach being used, but because of the their own personal qualities and/or the qualities of the relationship with their drugs worker.

any other setting, we will have been successful in engaging with clients who initially didn't want to cooperate. We can look to these cases in developing our own skills for dealing with the few people who give us a hard time.

7. Respect for the client's world view

We all have a fundamental need to be heard and understood, to be recognised and valued. SFBT respects and accepts the client's world view, rather than attempting to force an external interpretation on them (doing so would make it difficult if not impossible to maintain rapport and sustain a viable working relationship). On the other hand, matching and pacing the client's individual way of thinking and feeling will enhance rapport and actually help the client express themselves better. It is also likely to enhance their acceptance of the therapeutic relationship and lead to more productive outcomes.

Milton Erickson in his work, which has so greatly influenced brief therapies in general and SFBT in particular, stressed the importance of respecting both the client's rights, and their freedom to express themselves as they needed to (Zeig and Munion 1999). As a unique individual, of course, the client will have a singular view of the world which constitutes their reality. Though there may be times when this reality does not match either the therapist's ideas of what is 'right' for the client (or those of their family or the other people around them), it is paramount that the client's view is respected. Forthright as ever in his views on interacting with clients, Erickson did not mince his words: 'Sometimes, in fact, many more times than is realised, therapy can be firmly established on a sound basis only by the utilization of silly, absurd, irrational and contradictory manifestations' (Zeig and Munion 1999, p.44).

Accepting the client's reality means that we also agree to the problem they wish to work on, as it is described by them.[6] In so doing, we may also have to abandon our own views, if we have them, about what the problem 'really' is. If the client wishes to work on reducing his or her consumption of alcohol, then we help them determine a realistic and achievable goal resulting in drinking less. We must keep any theories we have about the underlying 'problem' to ourselves and focus on the

---

6   The obvious exception to this is where the client describes an illegal or totally unrealistic goal.

attainment of that goal. For example, in one of my demonstration videos the client speaks about her drinking problem, so that is what we focus on for the rest of the session. Observers regularly identify that she has underlying problems they would prefer to address, including repressed anger and relationship problems. This would not only disregard what the client has asked for, it would also complicate the whole process. Assuming that is, that the client stayed around to continue in the face of such a denial of her words.

The aim then is to enter the client's world and work from there, rather than attempting to get the client to accept some external reality which is imposed on them. We all tend to be more cooperative when we feel understood, and conversely can dig our heels in when our ideas or beliefs are not valued. The equivalent in therapy is to tell the client that their version of things is not real and that we have a better one (or greater insight, awareness or whatever).

8. Use time flexibly

As I have already mentioned, brevity is a consequence of SFBT, not its intent. Results are generally obtained over a few sessions because the focused way of working makes in more effective. But there should be no imperative to achieve results over a shorter or longer time frame than is required in any particular therapeutic relationship involving therapist, client, their given skills, circumstances and all the other variables that make each such alliance unique. Clients do not usually want to be part of an extended therapeutic relationship (Frank and Frank 1991), and it is implicit in the aims of therapy to encourage their autonomy and for the therapist to become redundant as soon as it is reasonable. These two aims therefore coincide by keeping it as brief as possible. SFBT takes the view that therapy should last only as long as it needs to: the notion of 'parsimony' permeates the approach (Berg and Miller 1992). In practice this generally translates into six sessions or fewer.

Though it is not the norm, in a few cases – for example where clients wish to attend to multiple difficulties or want support over an extended period – therapy may last months or even years. To illustrate the longer option, and that 'brief' does not necessarily mean 'quick', Bill O'Hanlon told me a story a few years ago:

> A guy came into my office waving a leaflet on my brief therapy seminars that he'd found in the waiting room. He was pretty upset. 'What's this brief therapy stuff,' he asked, 'How come you didn't do it with me? I've

been seeing you for two years.' I said, 'Your brief therapy has taken two years so far.' Different people need a different amount of time. (Winbolt 1996)

Berg and Dolan, in *Tales of Solutions* (2001), their excellent collection of SFBT case studies from around the world, tell the story of Steven who, with a long history of mental illness and a diagnosis of schizophrenia, was referred to a team using SFBT. It is a moving and inspiring account, the upshot of which is that the client attended 18 sessions over 29 months and achieved his main goals of getting a job and staying out of hospital. [7]

I have chosen to elaborate a little here because too great an emphasis on brevity can lead therapists to become preoccupied by their own sense of urgency and become too goal focused, rather than simply remaining solution focused, taking the process as it comes and using the minimum number of sessions necessary until the client is able to manage by themselves. That said, according to Jerome Frank, the duration of therapy is more likely to depend on the training of the therapist than the actual demands of the situation. Frank quotes Moshe Talmon to support this:

As with the frequency of sessions, the total duration of therapeutic contact seems to depend heavily on the expectations of the therapist. Thus, practitioners of long-term therapy, such as psychoanalysts, find that their patients take months or years to respond, while practitioners of forms of time-limited therapy, even therapy limited to a single session, obtain good results within their time frames. (Frank and Frank 1991, p.149).

The same ideas that inform the duration of therapy also govern the length of sessions. Though most people still stick to the 50–60 minute format, there is no requirement for this if the session appears to need more, or less, time. For practical purposes, of course, sessions are expected to last around an hour. But it happens that really effective therapy can happen early in the session and there is a natural 'end' that presents itself well before the hour is up. Experienced therapists I speak to can all identify times when they have reached these decisive moments, but where they have continued up to the full hour anyway, usually because of convention or because they did not want to 'short change' the client. Notwithstanding that it has come to be expected by all and sundry in the

---

7 The team was led by Joel Simon from Walden, New York, who contributed the case study.

healthcare system that sessions last an hour, it is impossible to get clients' rate of progress to fit exactly within this convention and we should allow ourselves the flexibility of working with the natural ebb and flow of each interaction. Prolonging the discussion beyond its useful life could turn a productive session into a less successful one. On the other hand, there may be times when a little extra time will make a big difference, and placing timekeeping ahead of the client's needs might mean missing an opportunity.

9. Give credit where it is due

The Italian philosopher Marsilio Ficino said that 'Praise derives its virtue not so much from the person who is giving it as from the one who is praised.' In other words, praise has the unsettling quality for the recipient of being difficult to totally ignore or reject. We generally receive too little affirmation in the form of compliments and praise once we have passed into adulthood (and sadly not before either for some children), despite the fact that we all know how much we crave this sort of recognition and how important it is for personal development, particularly in our early years.

Compliments are an integral part of the SFBT approach. Because of their therapeutic power, positive feedback, praise and affirmation are encouraging and compelling ingredients in successful therapy. Someone who is beset by their problems does not expect to hear that they are doing well in some aspects of their lives, even though their own outlook is understandably bleak. It can add balance to hear praise and other genuinely sincere and positive comments about their determination, successes (or attempts at success), good intentions and the other useful things they have done. When these observations are made by an experienced professional they add even more weight by helping the client understand that he or she is a capable, respectable and responsible member of society (Chaika 2000, p.147), and that their troubles are only part of who they are. The therapist should remark what he or she has learned about the positive aspects of the client's thinking, actions and intentions, and how these are useful resources in beginning to tackle the difficulties. Even with long-standing or apparently intractable problems people do some useful things some of the time, though they may not have recognised or taken credit for them.

Paying tribute to clients in this way is sometimes called 'cheerleading', a term that reflects its American origins. For it to be acceptable to the client, the use of compliments must naturally fit with the socially accepted levels of praise in the culture where it is being used. Outside the USA – particularly in the UK and the rest of Europe – people can be a little chary and even suspicious of tributes, especially if they appear too lavish. The habit must therefore be adjusted to fit not just the local climate but also individual clients' levels of comfort and acceptance.[8] Nevertheless the discreet use of complimentary language, appreciative expressions, surprise, inflections in the voice and appropriate gestures can all be used to effectively acknowledge and praise the client's efforts and successes. This will go a long way in enhancing rapport and developing the client's confidence. The therapist's positive reactions can be reassuring and also validate change, success or a certain course of action.

As in all other aspects of the interaction, here too the unique and individual attributes of the client play a part. Positive comments made by the therapist must 'fit' the client and be experienced by them as authentic, honest, relevant and genuine, even if unexpected. A respectful and competent therapist will use his or her listening and observation skills to gauge what is acceptable and comfortable for the client (Berg and Miller 1992).

What more is needed?

These 'building blocks' can be used as a starting point in the collaborative exercise of constructing solutions with the client. These will be expanded by specific techniques, such as setting goals, offering assignments, measuring progress and eliciting reports of success, that are covered in the following chapters. Taken as read are the intrinsic skills and abilities associated with the role of therapist or other professional. A sequence of steps or cluster of techniques does not in any way constitute therapy, any more than a collection of notes on a page constitutes music, so they are only regarded as a guide. Once they are assimilated into a way of thinking the technique becomes less important than the ongoing interaction with the client (Hawkes, Marsh and Wilgosh 1998).

In addition to the points above there are a few other considerations which tend to make therapy briefer and more successful. As we have seen the client's level of expectation is an important factor and it is part of the therapist's job to foster hope and expectancy. In SFBT this is done

---

8   How socially acceptable and trusted compliments are varies greatly even within the UK. Some regions and/or cultures are distinctly more suspicious and therefore less comfortable with ostentatious praise.

primarily through the use of enquiry for, as playwright Eugène Ionesco said, 'It is not the answer that enlightens, but the question.'

The questions clients ask themselves play an important part in creating and maintaining problems, as well as in resolving them (Goldberg 1998). Our aim, as therapists, should be to remain vigilant for the line of enquiry that will best facilitate the latter. This requires genuine curiosity, courage and above all creativity.

By the time they consult us about their difficulties most clients will already have gone over the problem in great detail, hashing and rehashing things to such a degree that when they start to tell us their story it can be a little like dropping a needle into the groove of a familiar record. By showing real curiosity about their situation, listening to their story and helping them to elaborate on it by enquiring about their coping skills, exceptions and other resources, we actively start to interrupt the familiar and limiting patterns they have fallen into and encourage new thinking about a chronic situation. To do this we have to be totally focused on the job in hand, listening and interacting with the client, rather than having conversations with ourselves about possible causes and contributions to their difficulties.

Resisting the siren song of our own theories and interpretations can be difficult especially for those of us who have been rigorously trained in the various assumptions which underpin the different models of therapy. With regard to doing SFBT, Berg and Miller (1992, p.1) actually went so far as to say: 'Those students least burdened with abstract theoretical notions are usually the most capable of learning solution focused therapy and, for that matter, therapy skills in general.'

I certainly find in my workshops that for some people the most difficult part of the whole SFBT equation is to sit and listen to the client's story without searching for some hidden meaning or striking out down a trail of their own invention. The straightforwardness of the approach seems to escape them. In essence we need to listen and respond to what the clients are telling us about what they want to change. We avoid looking for cause, searching for deeper meaning or pursuing our own interpretations in favour of identifying exceptions, success and resources and getting that first, small change to happen. Here too, SFBT offers pithy guidance in the form of the central philosophy: if it ain't broke, don't fix it; if it's not working, do something different; if it works, do more of it.

CHAPTER 6

The Language of Change

Language is the medium by which all understanding and interactions take place. It is also critical to the way our thought processes work and how our perceptions are formed. The words we use help to define our world and how we experience it. Doing effective therapy requires that we are extremely sensitive to these ideas so that we can help the client evade the traps that they, and we, may unwittingly be setting for themselves.

For therapists, therefore, the importance of understanding something about this process, and the relationship between the language we use and our perceptions, should not be overlooked. At the very least we must be aware of the role that language plays beyond the generally accepted idea that it simply enables us to 'talk'. 'Language' is not restricted to verbal transmissions from one person to another. We also have to consider the way we speak; tone, volume, emphasis, pitch, rhythm and so on, as well as non-verbal messages such as expression, posture, breathing and even those we less consciously register: pupil dilation, skin tone and perspiration.

Oddly, for a currency so widely used and valued as language, we actually spend very little time thinking about how we use it. In daily life this causes enormous problems as any of us knows. For professionals – whether in health, education, the law of any other of the lines of work where we can have an impact on the lives of others – it is worrying that so little attention is paid to how we listen and communicate.[1]

---

1   I know that many people have benefited from training in listening and communication skills, but these are usually add-ons to professional development courses of one sort or another. Since, in the caring professions (this includes medicine), language is a primary tool, it could feature more prominently in education of all kinds.

People and language are inseparable

In the quote that opens this chapter, Roger Lass, Professor of Linguistics at the University of Cape Town, describes the fundamental system of communication used by people everywhere (Lass 1987). His words resonated with me when I read them because it also perfectly reflects how we *use* language. Although we regularly employ our mother tongue without much thought for either the intricacies of the medium we are using or our relationship with it, language doesn't just describe our world, it also defines it, along with the limits we impose and possibilities that we allow ourselves (Haden Elgin 1999).

The statement at the start of this chapter, used here to describe language, can equally be used to explain us, the beings that use it. We are of course a reflection of our past history, in that our learnings, experiences and even those of previous generations will shape our way of interacting with the world, and our thoughts and actions in the present are unavoidably a prelude to the future.[2] There is even a school of thought which says that we only have our individual identities *because* of our language; being part of a language community means that we can name and describe ourselves as individuals (Brothers 1997).

There is no aspect of our lives which is untouched by language. It is our defining characteristic as a species and it provides the underpinnings of everything we do. We use it to create who we are, to protect our egos and to project an image of ourselves through how we narrate our lives to ourselves and others (Chaika 2000). It is even our badge of social identity (our accent, the jargon we use). Language cannot be separated from what it means to be human, and each of us uses it in our own unique way as we interact with ourselves and others. And yet we are generally neglectful of its real power to shape our awareness and expectations. Changing the language we use will change our experience.

'Perception and categorisation provide us with the concepts that keep us in touch with the world. Language extends that lifeline by connecting the concepts to words,' says Steven Pinker (2002, p.208). The key words here are 'perception' and 'categorisation'. Taking the line suggested by the Greek philosopher Epictetus (among others) that 'It is not the things themselves that worry us, but the opinions that we have about those

---

2   Since SFBT is about change, the focus is on the present and the future. Nothing can be done to change the past, but we can aim to influence behaviour in the present and the future.

things,' how we interpret an event will determine our thoughts and impressions of it. Or, put another way, and as we shall see later, what it means to us will affect how we react to it. Whether the glass is half full or half empty depends on how you interpret what you see when you look at the glass. To put this into context, a client who says 'My life is a total failure,' is likely to have a much bleaker outlook (from where they are sitting) than the client who can say 'My life has been really hard lately.'

Categorisation is important because it has such a large impact on our perceptions and how we interact with our surroundings. We automatically make certain assumptions about our world and then act according to them (Chaika 2000). These assumptions usually go unchallenged – by ourselves or by others – partly because they are outside our range of conscious awareness but also because this is one of the fundamental aspects of how language works. We can't keep stopping to examine the nuances and implications of the words and phrases we use. We take them for granted as we go about living our lives. For convenience we categorise people and things, and this habit underlies much of our vocabulary (dog, holiday, intelligent), our reasoning (I don't like dogs...) and even our behaviour (... so I stay away from them) (Pinker 1999).

If, when thinking about the death of a close relative, I put it into a category called 'Bad things that happen that ruin people's lives', I will have a different relationship with the event than if I put it in a category called 'Unpleasant but unavoidable events that are an inevitable part of life', or even 'Growth experiences'. This process has a direct link with what is known as explanatory style; the manner in which we habitually explain to ourselves why events happen (Seligman 1995). How we explain our experiences to ourselves – and in particular our problems – determines the hold they have over us, and what needs to be done to solve them (Furman and Ahola 1992). The way we think and talk about things determines for example whether they are fixed, unchangeable or permanent, or whether they are transitory, changeable or temporary. This in turn will affect how negative and pessimistic we are about change in our lives, or how hopeful or optimistic (Seligman 1995).

Language is the tool we use to do it, we can manipulate the language we use and thereby change our experience. Indeed, people have been doing just that throughout our history: 'The first technology of mood our ancestors discovered was language,' says Dylan Evans, 'People have used language in various ways to induce happiness.' He goes on to explain how humans have developed 'linguistic medicine' to help themselves feel better: a consoling chat, advice, encouragement and humour are among the examples. 'Words can be powerful antidepressants,' he says (Evans 2001, p.52). What we talk about and how we talk about it makes a difference, and it is such differences that can be used to make a difference to the client in SFBT (de Shazer 1994, p.10). Thus reframing a life seen as 'a total failure' into one that 'has been hard lately' makes a difference in how we discuss it, where we look for solutions, and even how motivated we are to do so.

I shall return to meaning at the end of this chapter. For now, Berg and Dolan (2001, p.175) have the final word. 'Even after all these years, we are still amazed at the virtually alchemical properties of language: how talking becomes the primary tool to spin the straw of problems into the gold of exceptions, solutions and ultimately a more satisfying quality of life.'

Do something different

In the next chapter I shall cover some of the principal ways language is used in SFBT. I want to emphasise its importance, and to show how uncomplicated the process of therapy can be once we and our clients think differently about their problems. To take up the metaphor used by Berg and Dolan again, if language is the thread that holds the client's life together, we want to unpick some of the tangles and rework it into something more serviceable.

There are three main lines of thought to this. The first is the need to be aware of the casual way we typically use language, where even our attempts at precision and clarity can simply make things worse.[3] When we recognise that meaning is attributed by the mind of the individual – rather than being a fixed and immutable quality of the words itself – we understand that there are as many meanings as there are

---

3   The fact that we can define a large number of words is not a guarantee that we know anything about the objects or operations they stand for. Definitions are abstract. Though we have a common understanding about what terms like 'tree' or 'depression' mean, we do not know from these abstract terms what the tree in Jason's garden looks like or what Indira's depression feels like to her. Attempts to define 'trees' or 'depression' more clearly generally lead to 'a hopeless snarl' unless we give specific examples of what we are talking about (see Hayakawa 1990).

people; the person using the word may not mean the same thing as the person hearing it.

The second point relates to how words, or more precisely the meanings we attribute to them, affect our experience. Without going into it too deeply here, words carry more with them than simply the dictionary definitions (which we also oversimplify by calling them 'meaning'). They bring with them a wealth of connotations far beyond the agreed descriptions. Furthermore, one of the reasons that this process is so powerful is that it is largely involuntary; meanings attach themselves to words and whether I like it or not, when I hear (or think) a word I must experience my meaning for it. As author and professor of psychiatry Leslie Brothers (1997, p.4) says 'When I hear a word in a language I know, it is not possible for me to hear just the sounds, I am compelled to experience the meaning of the word, its semantic aspect.'

The third line to this discussion involves the specific tactics and devices – known as 'solution-talk' from a phrase coined by Steve de Shazer – which enable us to stay on track and ensure that therapy is as effective as possible.

How we employ language – the way it influences not just our world view but also how we experience our lives – is a subject too vast to cover in any real detail here. But we cannot ignore it – to do so would be to commit the same error that causes people to get stuck with their problems in the first place and so perpetuate their difficulties.

We all know what we mean...or do we?

The meanings we attribute to the things that occur in our lives are defined by the language we employ to think about them, and the words we use to describe them to ourselves and others. So far so good. But as we have all found to our cost when a major misunderstanding occurs, communicating that meaning to others can be a perilous business, due to the abstract nature of language. We take for granted that something said is something understood, and we are constantly overestimating how much we actually communicate (Minsky 1987, p.67).

The actual terms and expressions we use as we describe our experience to ourselves fix that experience for us, and mediate how we perceive and respond to it. So, to be an 'alcoholic' brings with it all the baggage, beliefs and ramifications of the term.[4] For example, there are legions of people (including Alcoholics Anonymous) whose view of alcoholism is that it is a disease from which the sufferer never fully recovers. On the other hand, using another term will alter the perceptions of both the sufferer and those around them (therapist included). Changing the description, say, to that of 'a person wanting to change their drinking habit' immediately reframes the situation, empowers both client and therapist *and* suggests a course of action.[5]

Labels are fine, we need them to talk to our clients, to think about their problems and in discussions with colleagues about our clients. The trouble arises when we forget that these labels are merely a linguistic device and start to mistake the description ('alcoholic' in this case) for the person or their activities.[6] Labels help us recognise patterns of behaviour but should not be mistaken for the people doing that behaviour.

> Finding a name for something is a way of conjuring its existence, or making it possible for people to see a pattern where they didn't see one before... We think and behave the way we do in large part because we have words that make these thoughts and behaviours possible...
> (Rheingold 1988, cited in Elgin 2000, p.57)

All that is needed to start the process of change is first to see how limiting the descriptions we use can be and second to remember to see the person rather than the description that has attached itself to them. This is not to say that some problems are not extremely challenging or tough to deal with, or to deny the very real difficulties in some people's lives. However, the sooner we start to ask the right questions about precisely *how* the client experiences their difficulties (as opposed to asking what the difficulties are), the better. It will introduce the client to new ways of thinking, and suggest strategies that will render therapy both more effective and more efficient.

---

4   I have chosen alcoholism here as an example. The same applies to any description, especially diagnostic labels: depression, anxiety, dysfunctional, ADHD...take your pick.

5   For a whole book on this topic see Berg and Miller 1992.

6   Mistaking the map for the territory as Korzybski so famously put it.

It starts with a question

Questions are the basis of any therapeutic interview and SFBT follows this convention, with a difference. This process is structured around carefully constructed questions designed not just to elicit a reply but also to provoke an internal response in the client. Sometimes, SFBT therapists will even ask questions without expecting a reply (see the Questions section on pp.74–76)

Clients are frequently not very clear about why the problem is a problem for them. That is, they will say that they feel bad, are having panic attacks or arguing with their spouse or whatever, and although at a surface level it may seem evident that this is a difficulty, until we, and they, understand what is problematic about it we won't be able to tackle it by negotiating a solvable problem (O'Hanlon and Weiner-Davis 1989). After all, to use the last example, all couples have disagreements and many argue vociferously. Few would say they like it, but most manage to navigate this almost inevitable part of conjugal bliss without describing it as a problem with which they need professional help. So what is it that makes arguing in our client's relationship a problem for them? Chances are that it is not the arguing that is really causing them grief, but the feelings they have about the conflict, the ensuing feelings of hurt, being misunderstood, insecurity or whatever. Or, it may be that their arguing upsets the children or is simply spoiling the quality of their lives. I am not diminishing the destructiveness of some kinds or arguing, it can be quite hot emotionally and very distressing, but in itself it is usually not the problem.[7] Indeed, couples that are generally satisfied with their relationships actually build repair mechanisms into their arguments to limit the damage (Gottman 1993). And, although it could be argued that they might find a less stressful and demanding way of airing their grievances, it fulfils a vital function for most of them. As one of the leading researchers on the matter says: 'What separates contented couples from those in deep marital misery is a healthy balance between their positive and negative feelings and actions toward each other' (Gottman 1998). So the negative aspects of the argument are compensated for by other aspects of their behaviour.

SFBT, in seeking out the exceptions, will naturally and conversationally build on the positive aspects of the interactions anyway, but in order to

---

7 It is not arguing per se that damages relationships. It is lack of respect, hostility and contempt that cause misery and eventual breakdown (see Gottman et al. 1976).

structure the sessions and guide the process something more is needed; we'll need to question our client about what is they want to change.

Negotiating a solvable problem

In order to tackle a problem effectively it must first be described with reasonable clarity. In solution focused parlance this means 'negotiating a solvable problem'. Once this has been done, some kind of solution – or at least a course of action – usually starts to become apparent. Solution building in SFBT doesn't focus on problems, it works at eliciting clients' descriptions of what they want to be different, how they want their lives to be. Nevertheless, when they arrive at our door most clients are preoccupied with their problems, so this is a reasonable and respectful place to start.

But simply accepting the client's declaration that there is a problem or even their description of it is unlikely to be much help. After all, they will have been asking themselves questions and providing answers without success. In fact, most don't realise that many of the questions they ask, both consciously and unconsciously, lie at the heart of their discontent (Goldberg 1998). They are not likely to get the change they seek if we simply do more of the same. We will need to ask the right questions; questions that are related to action and change.

Orienting questions

We are surrounded by questions in our lives and a great many of them go unanswered. The reason for this is that they are poorly designed. As scientists so often like to remind us, the quality of the responses you get is dictated by the quality of questions you ask. Competent researchers know they have to ask the right questions otherwise the data they gather will be useless to them. It has often been said that what distinguishes the true scientist is not to be able to come up with answers; it is his or her ability to state the problem, to frame questions, so that the relevant facts can be uncovered. Psychologist, speech pathologist and author Wendell Johnson, reflecting half a century ago on the quandaries of 'unhappy and inefficient people' said:

> Now, intimate personal problems are not greatly different from problems in the laboratory. Before they can be solved, they must be stated. Before helpful answers can be got, suitable questions must be asked... What the

maladjusted person cannot do – and what he (or she) must learn to do – is to specify the sort of answers he needs. This is a way of saying that he (or she) has a conspicuous lack of ability to ask questions that would be relaxing, or satisfying or adjustive.' (Johnson 1946, p.17)

Therapists often overlook how their style of questioning will determine the kind of answers they get. For a simple example, take a look at Figure 6.1. It clearly illustrates how the question we ask will decide the route the conversation takes.

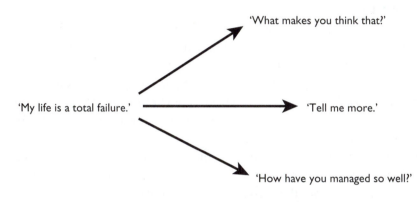

Figure 6.1 The style of questions we use will determine the kind of answers we get.

If, in response to the client's statement 'My life is a total failure', we come up with 'Tell me more', we are of course acknowledging their statement in a respectful way. We are also likely to produce a linear dialogue that is unlikely to stray from a litany of life's problems. If on the other hand, we try something a little more adventurous, we might say 'What makes you think that?' Note that this still implicitly acknowledges the client's statement, but adds something more. In order to respond the client *has to do something different* to come up with the answer. He or she will have to think a little and supply the supporting evidence for their statement which, quite evidently, cannot be accepted as it stands (no life can be a 'total' failure). So in asking for the evidence we also offer a gentle challenge.

Or, we might ask a truly solution focused question along the lines of 'How have you managed so well so far?' This still respects the client's statement by apparently accepting it, but it offers a wealth of other possibilities as well. It goes straight to the heart of looking for exceptions and resources; it suggests that the client is in some way coping despite the problem; it focuses the client on their 'successes' rather than the failures;

it challenges the client's use of the word 'total'; it changes the focus of the conversation from problem to solution focused.

Each of these three responses will take the conversation in a completely different direction. Furthermore, some of those directions will be more empowering for the client than others, and the response 'Tell me more', will contribute to little or nothing in the way of progress, and may even do harm, by encouraging the client to introspect.

Opening doors

Marilee Goldberg, in her book *The Art of the Question* (1998, p.5) says, 'It is important for clients to learn that the solutions they seek lie behind doors which could remain forever closed unless opened by the right questions.' Steve de Shazer and his team developed generic questions, offered as tasks to be used, regardless of the client's presenting problem, as 'skeleton keys' to unlock change in a wide variety of situations (de Shazer 1985). Walter and Peller developed a matrix of questions designed to invite respondents into a different area of thinking. These difference-oriented questions act as 'Invitations to clients to loosen old restrictive beliefs or rules they have about themselves or their experience and to create more useful beliefs.' (Walter and Peller 1992, p.177)

Questions form the basis of therapy. They may be the questions our clients ask themselves, those they ask us and the ones we ask them. Many are unspoken. They are the internal questions we all have, some we are consciously aware of, others we are not. The difficulties that bring people into therapy will be reflected in and generated by their internal dialogue and especially their internal questions (Goldberg 1998). There will be many questions our clients have never asked and, since those that they *have* been asking themselves have not produced the type of helpful answers they seek, then it is the therapist's job to break the pattern by asking new questions that expand the client's options, to 'stimulate a fresh look at the same old picture' (Berg and Dolan 2001, p.3).

The creative use of questions is something that takes practice and a certain degree of confidence. SFBT prescribes some particular forms of questions as you'll see later in this chapter but these are only starting points. The real work is done through the therapist's constant creativity in generating the questions they use. But, like all creative endeavours, it is not something that can be practised in our heads. The creative process only happens when we are doing something.[8] We cannot rehearse creativity because, in therapy, it is a product of the interaction with the client. So, there are no 'great' questions. As de Shazer (1994, pp.97–98) says: 'A question can only become "great" when it precedes a "great answer". A "great answer" is judged to be "great" only when it is useful to the purpose of therapy.'

Questions are the essential tool for doing the groundwork in SFBT. The greater the skill we develop in the art of designing and using questions creatively the better the results will be. In conversations in general we pay little attention to how we structure our enquiries; the formulae we use tend to be routine and habitual. In therapy, and in SFBT in particular, this will not do. The questions we use will determine where the interaction goes and what we learn on the way. The client carries the seeds of the solution with them, it is said. If we are to help those seeds germinate and grow then we need to do something more than ask the common-or-garden type of questions like: 'How are you?', 'What do you feel about that?', 'When will you be ready to get back to work?', or 'How would you like your partner/mother/son to behave towards you?'

Much more could be said about questions but since we all bring our unique skills and talents to the relationship it is certainly more useful to encourage you to practise, than to memorise lists of 'form' questions. I encourage budding and more experienced therapists to experiment with questions and observe responses as they go about their daily lives. This helps build creativity and flexibility in the use of language and thence confidence and familiarity. I also think that understanding what a given question is intended to *do* before using it helps to focus our thinking as well as our conversational style.

Solution-talk versus problem-talk

The concept of 'solution-talk' as opposed to 'problem-talk' refers to conversational tactics used in SFBT to uncover resources and construct solutions. The idea is best described in a de Shazer story I have paraphrased here:

---

8 This is why many people find they cannot write, they wait for inspiration to strike before starting work. But inspiration or the creative process is a product of actively engaging in work, i.e. starting to write. Authors will often say that their characters decide the outcome.

Imagine spending half an hour talking to your client about all the problems in their life, focusing particularly on their feelings of depression. How do you, and they, feel at the end of the half hour? By contrast, imagine spending thirty minutes talking in a focused way about all the things that have gone well in his or her life, showing particular interest in their feelings of success. How do you both feel after that half hour?

When I get people in my workshops to do a shortened (twenty-minute) version of this exercise there is – unsurprisingly – a marked difference between parts one and two. In the first part participants tell me that details pile up, negativity increases and very soon they can't see the wood for the trees. The result for the therapist is that they start to feel overwhelmed, confused and discouraged; they feel beset by the size of the problem as they start to 'buy in' to the client's sense of hopelessness.

When we shift the emphasis to solution-talk they tell me that things feel lighter, they discover strengths and resources they had not seen before, and the likelihood of moving forward seems more tangible and real. They also start to think more optimistically about the possibilities of a solution to the problem. Some 'clients' even report that this short conversation has shifted their whole perception, and that they can now see their way forward.

Something that I notice as I watch the group doing this exercise is even more revealing. While understandably they are at first a little hesitant in exploring this new way of talking to others, gradually the buzz in the room intensifies as the conversations pick up. The atmosphere becomes more relaxed and there is often laughter. Most interesting for me is that as I watch the couples working, I see their body language start to change; they become more animated, shoulders straighten, faces look more comfortable. It is also much harder to interrupt their conversations as I try to get the group's attention at the end of this second part of the exercise.

Using solution-talk does not mean that we exclude problems from the discussion. Clients need and expect to discuss what ails them and it would seem churlish and lacking in respect to deny them the opportunity. We can also learn a lot by listening to their problems. Rather than passively listening to a catalogue of woes, however, or conducting an uninterrupted investigation into problems, we can respond in a solution focused way. In our questions and summaries as the conversation progresses we can begin complimenting the client on their resilience, identifying exceptions and searching for resources. So, even when having a problem focused conversation with our clients we can remain resolutely solution focused in our thinking.

Solution-talk, according to Walter and Peller, relies on four assumptions to guide that thinking:

- a focus on the positive, the solution, the future facilitates change in the desired direction

- exceptions to *every* problem can be created by therapist and client, that can be used to build solutions

- change is happening all the time

- meaning and experience are intellectually constructed.

(1992, p.63–64)

The sooner that solution-talk is initiated in the process the better. Studies have shown that when it occurs early in the process, change happens sooner, therapy is shorter and treatment is more likely to be continued and completed (Lipchik 2002).

Process versus content

When listening to our clients it is very easy to become absorbed in the story they are telling us. As the narrative progresses, though, it can quickly begin to appear so complicated that it is difficult to know where to start. It may even seem as though their situation is just so problematic that we begin to get as bogged down as they are by the intricacies of their stories. When this happens it is generally because we have been listening only to the content and ignoring the process.

Content concerns the detail of the narrative, the who-said-what-to-whom, the intricate aspects as seen and reported by the client. It covers the events that have occurred, the concrete 'facts', and usually includes the 'problem' as the client sees it. Since content must, by definition, relate to things that have happened in the past, it is also unchangeable.

Process, on the other hand, refers to the interactions between people: the *how* rather than the *what*. Clients are usually unaware of the process, of how they are responding to their problem and life in general. Listening for process means being attentive to the actions and interactions in the client's life. Since the primary focus is therefore on what is happening – rather than what was said, thought or felt – it is easier to talk about change, to identify new possibilities and encourage a different course of action.

Content tends to limit possibilities because it is defined and fixed (it has already happened). Process reveals possibilities because it is ongoing and continuous, it works in the here and now and will remain open to influence in the future. SFBT focuses on ways of changing harmful or limiting patterns of behaviour. In enquiring about process the therapist invites the client to take an observer's stance in viewing the situation they want to change. This brings with it another advantage for the client; it increases their sense of empowerment or personal agency (Freedman and Combs 1996). When talking about the detail of an event (content) the client must be intimately involved in the narrative in such a way that it is difficult to view the situation objectively. Asking about patterns of interaction, the steps they took, the actions of those around them and their responses (process), will elicit behavioural descriptions. From this vantage point it is easier to plan the steps that can lead the client towards solutions.

So, when I was working with a 12-year-old boy who was sent to me by his parents because he was absconding from school, the detail described by his mother ('He is unhappy', 'he just disappears', 'doesn't come back', 'no one knows where he is', 'breaks the rules', 'flouts authority'...) provided useful information, but was less helpful in changing the behaviour. I could have explored all these things with him but I knew it would lead to an impasse. After all, it was a safe bet that those were the conversations that parents and staff were already having with him and if it had been effective I would not have been involved. Doing something different and asking about the process provided suggestions for a new course of action. ('What was happening on the days you walked out?' 'Who was with you?' 'What were they doing?' and most importantly of all 'What happened on the days you stayed in school?' 'How did you manage that?' 'When is it not a problem?'). From questions like these we learned that he stayed in school more often than he left; that when a particular situation occurred – he felt that a particular staff member was picking on him – his only course of action was to leave; that he was resourcefully using a strategy, as he saw it, to keep himself safe rather than deliberately acting disobediently.

Giving emphasis to the process does not mean ignoring content entirely, that would be neither possible or desirable since the two are complementary. The things that the client tells us about their situation certainly should not be dismissed and I would never wish to give the impression that such details are not important; they certainly are to the client. It is essential that we listen to their story, to understand their beliefs, thoughts and feelings about a given situation or event. It is the content that brings vitality, detail and intensity to the narrative as well as helping us see things from the client's perspective. As psychiatrist and therapist Irvin Yalom (1989, p.188) says: 'Details are wonderful. They are informative, they are calming and they penetrate the anxiety of the problem: the patient feels that, once you have the details, you have entered into his life.' Thus content will also provide information about problem free times, exceptions and other resources. But we should not allow ourselves to be over reliant on it.

The point here is that we need to be aware of the distinction between process and content, to listen for both, and to be able to choose which we focus on in our questions, and to understand why we are doing it. So while we are naturally talking about content we are thinking and enquiring about process.

Finally, I have observed in my own work, and also in the cases that other therapists discuss with me in supervision and workshops, that we are far more likely to get stuck when we are caught up in the content. Just as our clients frequently get hamstrung by analysing and ruminating on the intricacies of their situations, therapists too can become ensnared by these details. Questions about process, on the other hand, always provide information that can lead to action, change or reappraisal. An example would probably help here:

> Pam came to see me because, in her words, she was drinking too much. Her husband, George, was suffering from a degenerative disease that would eventually mean he would need full time professional care. For the time being though he was living at home with her. Although she had regular contact with the social services – indeed they were encouraging her to move her husband to a residential care home as soon as possible – she was attending to all his needs. This meant round the clock, unremitting and demanding work. On top of the physical and emotional burden of Pam's situation, the nature of George's illness also meant that he was rarely the old George she had married 25 years earlier. He had sudden mood swings, was developing a violent temper, was verbally abusive and, even though he was confined to a wheelchair, he often struck out at her, particularly when he was tired.
>
> All in all, Pam had been living a pretty thankless life for the past five years and it was getting worse. Despite the help that had been offered,

Pam was adamant that she would continue to look after George herself for as long as possible and that meant 'at least another year'. Accepting the offer of residential care for him was simply not an option and she would not be moved from that position.

The one moment of relief in Pam's routine came when she got George to bed each evening. Once he was in bed he would watch TV until he dropped off and this usually meant that from about 7.30 her time was more or less her own. One evening a week she had someone come and sit for her and she went out ballroom dancing with her friends. She also went to church meetings fairly regularly and had good social support from a small network of friends.

The problem, Pam said, was that her drinking was out of control and that if she didn't do something about it she would soon be no use to either George or herself. She painted a dramatic picture of decline into helpless dependency on alcohol. Given the apparent gravity of the situation I was surprised to learn just how this problem manifested itself. Each evening (as it turned out not *every* evening), once Pam had got George off to bed she would sit down, turn on the TV and open a bottle of wine. 'And I always finish the bottle,' she said. 'Once that bottle has been opened it is impossible for me to stop drinking until I have finished it.'

Pam felt that she was becoming a slave to alcohol. The most alarming thing about it, she said, was that her inability to stop until the bottle was finished demonstrated how weak she really was. In fact this weakness was for her more of a problem than the drinking; she was being controlled by her habit and was surely destined to ruin her life. So convinced was she of this that all my efforts to reframe the situation, to get her to lighten up on herself a little, were rejected out of hand.

I tried in vain to persuade her that her devotion to George demonstrated strength, not weakness, that given her situation a few drinks in the evening might be a normal coping strategy, that one bottle an evening (she never opened a second) did not constitute a ruined life. Pam was unmoved. I tried a different tack; naturally she loved her husband and wanted to do the best for him. Was it really best for George that she continue to struggle to look after him at home? Wouldn't he be better off with professional care? Wouldn't their relationship actually improve if she could visit him as a wife by freeing herself of the role of carer and keeper?

Exploring these content issues only seemed to convince Pam that I had not listened, had not really understood her story. What was important to her, and the reason she came to see me in the first place she insisted, was that she had 'no control' over her drinking. She was not interested in my suggestions, in a new perspective, or in the idea that, hard though it was to accept, she could actually provide better care for George in a professional setting. She made it clear to me that what she wanted from therapy was to change her drinking habit, nothing else. Had I tried the more conventional route by exploring what lay behind the need to hang onto George, or her fear of not being in control, I think she would have run a mile. I could have pursued those ideas, or the way she stubbornly refused my suggestions that, though it was not a long-term solution, a little drink might be a normal response to the extreme demands of her situation and therefore a temporary rather than permanent problem. To have done so would not only have alienated her from me it would have been disrespectful.

Stop for a moment and think about how you view Pam's prospects and the questions you could ask her. As we listen to our clients, empathise with them and offer our support it is easy to be drawn into their story with them and so lose sight of our primary role as agent for change. It is tempting and even natural to allow the direction of the discourse to be determined by the client. This will usually produce more and more detail to a point where we can become mired in the content and 'can't see the wood for the trees'.

So I turned to the process: were there any evenings when she did not finish the bottle? How was it that she did not need to open a second bottle? Were there any times, however rare, when she had done something different in the evenings, rather than taking that first drink? What was her social life like? What was she doing during the day that she did not drink? Quite quickly an image emerged of Pam as a far more resourceful woman than she had led me to believe. Furthermore, as she answered me her body language started to change; she started to sit up a little more, became more engaged in our conversation and a little more animated.

What I learned was that Pam had good social support, she was active in her church despite the demands on her at home and that someone regularly sat with George to provide respite when she needed it. I also discovered that she was passionate about ballroom dancing (she and George had been regular dancers until his illness prevented it). One evening a week, every week, Pam went out dancing with her friends and, although there was a bar, she never drank! In fact Pam was not a social drinker. She drank alone at the end of a hard day. Pretty soon Pam's story had taken on some added dimensions. Far from the hopeless out-of-control binge drinker she had attempted to describe to me, by her own description she was a woman who, notwithstanding her personal difficulties, was managing to keep some much needed balance in her life.

She enjoyed her friendships, she protected her social routine, there was more to Pam than George's wife and carer.

These process questions not only showed up the exceptions to the problem – the times when Pam did not drink – we also found out that Pam's enemy was isolation. When she was with other people she did not drink. All these points were given added vitality since, whatever her wishes and sooner rather than later, she would be living alone.

Rather than attacking the drinking directly we approached Pam's search for solutions by building on her resources: her social support, lifestyle and interests. Helped by a new awareness of the pattern in her drinking she was able to now view it as a response to her demanding situation rather than an indication of inevitable decline. She also began to accept the idea of George's eventual move to residential care. By our third session she had achieved her goal of spending an evening at home without drinking. Added benefits were that she was feeling better about herself generally and was looking further ahead in her planning. During our fourth session Pam mentioned that she thought the relationship between George and herself had improved a little, that the pressure due to her situation was less demoralising and that she thought she could manage without me from here on.

Confusing meaning with purpose

Clients, and sometimes their therapists, also manage to bamboozle themselves by confusing meaning with purpose. Socrates famously said 'The unexamined life is not worth living,' and most of us spend a good deal of our lives trying to attribute meaning to events, our actions, the actions of others and so on. Even the least introspective person, as they traverse particularly trying stages of their lives will ask themselves 'What's it all about?' One of the natural attributes of the human mind is the search for meaning. And a noble pastime it is too, given that many of the most influential people in history have been philosophers. On a personal level we could not function without the capacity to search for meaning and come up with plausible explanations to calm our anxieties. But there are times when we feel our lives are short on meaning, or that the meaning lacks the impetus we feel we need. What then?

I am not going to attempt to tackle the timeless and unsettling question, 'What is the meaning of life?' That is the province of philosophy and a question that has been wrestled with down the ages by people far better equipped to ask it than I. We all grapple with these existential questions from time to time and some clients even come into therapy searching for meaning. It is precisely because the search for meaning is such a universal quest, and the answer (if that is the right word) is likely to be so personal and ephemeral that therapy, brief or otherwise, is not able to resolve things definitively. That is not to say that we cannot reflect on these points with our clients and even provide them with some tools for thinking about the question. But it serves us all well to untangle our own thinking around meaning and purpose, because we often confuse the two. Searching for meaning in things – though it might be a commendable pastime – is quite different from attempting to instil purpose. Lou Marinoff, professor of philosophy and a therapist, elaborates the point in this way:

> Purpose is an ultimate object or end to be attained. It is a goal, Meaning has to do with how you understand your life on an ongoing basis. Meaning is in the way things happen, not necessarily in the end result. Understanding depends on experience, and meaning – like experience – is very personal. (1999, p.210)

He uses the example of a restaurant menu; its purpose is to help you make a choice about what to eat, the meaning is to provide information about those choices. 'If you are in a restaurant in France and you don't understand a word of French, then the menu will be meaningless to you – even though you know its purpose.'

A better-known example is that of philosopher Alfred Korzybski, who cautioned that the map is not the territory. The purpose of a map is to show me the lie of the land, to enable me to plan my trip and arrive at my destination, but it is only a symbolic representation of the terrain it describes. The meaning of the map, on the other hand, will vary according to my intentions; the same map will have different meanings for the tourist and the railway engineer. So purpose might be likened to function, and function is generally verifiable. The purpose of a fork in Western cultures is to enable us to eat without putting our fingers in the food, but the meaning…?

Of course, not many of us lie awake at night worrying about the meaning of a fork. But people do have their sleep disturbed, and far more besides, in their futile ruminations on meaning, as if it were a fixed and definable quality. Meaning, like beauty, is in the eye of the beholder. Events do not have meaning in themselves, it is ascribed by the observer or participant in an event, not the other way around (Walter and Peller 1992). To apply the example to human relationships, the purpose of two people meeting may be to have a conversation, but the same event will differ in meaning according to the setting. Coming together in the therapy room will not signify the same thing as coming together in a police cell or a honeymoon suite. The meaning of the interaction will be different for each participant, and according to the setting. By contrast the purpose in each case is unlikely to be so obscure, at least in the second two examples. Clarity of purpose in the therapy setting is the aim of the process and one of the reasons I am writing this paragraph.

We all need meaning but we should not allow ourselves to become mesmerised by that need. If we keep in mind that meaning is constructed by the individual, that it is relative to their experience and interactions, and that it evolves and changes constantly, we can avoid being incautiously snagged by the confusion between meaning and purpose. Searching for and discussing meaning, while perfectly valid in some situations (therapy included), will not advance the process as quickly as identifying purpose. Quite the opposite; it is very often the relationship between the client and their meanings that is causing the problem. Take for example the common trick of making ourselves feel bad with the 'causal equivalent': 'I failed the exam so this means I am a failure'. The meaning ('I am a failure') we give to the event ('failed the exam') determines how we feel about the event and how we subsequently think and act. (For more on causal equivalents see Battino and South 1999.)

There are two possible routes out of this impasse. We can come up with new meanings (see Reframing in Chapter 7), or we can recognise how meaning can deceive us and focus on purpose: 'I need to cheer myself up', 'I need to resit the exam', or whatever.

Purpose relates to attaining goals, ends and objectives, meaning has to do with how we understand our lives. The two are probably inseparable, they are certainly indispensable to healthy and balanced living, but they are not the same. In the words of a popular saying, 'The purpose of life is a life of purpose'.

Core themes of therapy and change

I started this chapter by referring to the language we use and the link with our perceptions. In discussing meaning I have come full circle. Language, perception and meaning: these fundamental facets of life are also the core themes of therapy and change.

Our ability to communicate as we do is what sets us apart as a species but that gift is double-edged. On the one hand we are able to convey and infer infinite shades of meaning, on the other hand we are often tripped up by our apparent lack of understanding of how we allow ourselves to be influenced and our experience shaped by our language. Change the language and we inevitably change the experience. If we agree that the words we use stand for the things they describe – they are symbols that represent the things not the things themselves – then we also must accept that we have unlimited freedom in how we choose to use those representations.

The levels of abstraction we use in our daily lives serve us well and need not be a hindrance. As long as we are functioning as we would wish we need not devote too much thought to these matters. But when unhappy or in difficulty we do need to consider them, and what better way than to review the way we represent them to ourselves in thought and language. We usually cannot change the events themselves but we can change how we think about, view and discuss those events both with others and with ourselves.

A major advantage in exploring the significance of language in therapy is that it heightens our conscious awareness of what is really going on in the interaction. In the words of Elaine Chaika (2000, p.vii), 'One literally learns to hear more, to listen more deeply and to make more connections.' Greater sensitivity to our client's speech therefore means increasing the effectiveness of the therapeutic interaction.

There is widespread and tacit approval for the view that when someone has a problem the difficulty lies with them, that they are somehow faulty or dysfunctional. SFBT asks us to reconsider this by framing problems as a malfunction in our interactions (with others, with ourselves) rather than evidence of a faulty personality, pathology or suchlike. This shift of focus provides a pathway that will lead to greater clarity and empowerment. In the next chapter I will outline the linguistic accessories that we have at our disposal to do this.

CHAPTER 7

The Use of Language in Therapy

I have taken a little time on exploring the significance of language in therapy because of its fundamental importance. It is the medium we use to explain things to ourselves and it has long been recognised that even psychiatric illness can result from limited or distorted thinking (Watzlawick 1978). Since language and thinking are inextricably linked and both are hugely implicated in psychological well-being, helping our clients develop a less constricting mental vocabulary and encouraging greater flexibility in how they think will start to show them the way out of their difficulties. When the responses and actions they habitually use don't work for them it is time for them to do something different. Flexibility is the key here; it is no good just having options, they also have to know they have them and be ready to exercise them as needed.

What goes for the client is also true for the therapist or helper. In order to enable the client to develop more effective habits of language and thought we have first to cultivate them in ourselves. This starts, as Elaine Chaika says above, with heightening our own linguistic awareness. Against this background SFBT provides a number of verbal devices we can use in conversations with our clients. These are the subject of this section.

Nobody generally argues with the idea that as helpers it is useful, even essential, to be acutely sensitive to the language our clients use. Equally, we can all see the importance of developing our own language skills for the benefit of our clients. But I have noticed that as people develop an interest in SFBT and start to become comfortable with the medium, many seem to lose confidence or doubt their abilities in this area. Apprehension when studying something new is natural and understandable, and part of the learning process. Learning the language of SFBT is like learning any other language (though much simpler than actually learning a foreign tongue!). It takes practice, repetition, willingness to learn and time. In this section I have included several exercises to develop these habits so that solution focused skills can become part of your repertoire.

Devices and gizmos

I struggle with how to describe what I have called 'verbal devices'. This term sounds horribly detached from the subtle and intricate interplay of conversation, and expressions like tools, gambits, strategies and so on all have connotations of mechanics, manipulation or planning not suited to the job. I need a word that says 'a temporary tool, gadget or idea to fit the task in hand' so in my workshops I have settled on the term 'gizmo'. What I want to convey is the multi-faceted, fluid, free play of language and ideas that transform a discussion into conversation. In so doing we move from discussing 'events' where the client merely reports their experience to a more lively and creative exercise marked by sincere interest, curiosity and creativity. Conversations in SFBT engender a spirit of collaborative exploration; they seek every opportunity to create new possibilities for the client.

Some of these so-called gizmos are conversational gambits that most people use in their daily lives anyway. Others require a little more practice to become familiar with them. Either way, solution focused practitioners recognise the value of taking an active stance in choosing the language that they use. As Bill O'Hanlon says: 'Language has a way of reifying, solidifying certain views of reality. It can be used as a tool to question unhelpful realities. So we have learned to be very careful about the way we use language in therapy' (O'Hanlon and Weiner-Davis 1989, p.60).

The way we speak to clients, both in terms of what we say and how we say it, has a major impact. SFBT practitioners recognise this and actively employ language to help the client towards finding their own solutions. The way in which helpers and therapists speak can introduce distinctions that will be helpful to their clients and eliminate those that aren't, we can identify and help correct limiting distortions, and we can work with our clients to develop an awareness of their habits of thought and speech. These are, after all, the only media we have to help them make and maintain the changes they seek (Battino and South 1999; O'Hanlon and Weiner-Davis 1989).

A simple way to make these gizmos habitual is to start with one or two and try them out. Try them with your clients or patients and see how they react. Probably you are using some of these already. For example, Normalising and Reframing (see below) are certainly devices most of us are accustomed to using, though we don't necessarily think of them by those names, in fact most people use them without thinking of them at all.

Normalising

To speak about the concern as if it is in the realm of normal human
experience, rather than an exotic or terrible thing. (O'Hanlon and Beadle 1994, p.40)

Normalising brings the client's difficulty into the realm of human experience. It makes the shift from simplistic or pathological labels towards more normal and confidence inspiring explanations.

Speaking about clients' concerns as though they are within the normal range of life events – rather than dramatic and exceptional – can help to lessen their anxieties about being odd, crazy, an outsider or doomed. People often think that they are the only person in the world with their particular problem but when they understand that others have suffered in the same way and that their problem or symptoms can be described in normal everyday terms, they begin to feel less of a 'freak' and more able to discuss their problem. Normalising is the opposite of pathologising or catastrophising.

For example, most parents worry at various times about some aspect of their children's behaviour or development, until they speak to other parents who report the same quirks in their own kids. It can be reassuring to discover that other people's children can be defiant and rebellious, faddy eaters or TV addicts and that the behaviour of our own offspring is a normal phase and does not necessarily predict a career as a failure or a delinquent (with all the attendant implications for our parenting).

In its simplest form normalising means responding in a matter-of-fact way to the information our clients present. Think of the different styles of the British press. The tabloids present the information as though disaster is at hand, the broadsheets, typically, will present the same story in a less dramatic fashion. Both are news, but one goes for impact, the other for information. O'Hanlon and Weiner-Davis (1989, p.94) say 'We tend to offer commonplace explanations at every opportunity and a great many of the client's 'news items' are shrugged off as simply "not newsworthy".' Another writer, Wendell Johnson, in his classic *People in Quandaries*, points out how discussing other situations, similar to that of the client, can be helpful, because it demonstrates that '[the client's] own misery is neither unique, mysterious nor unacceptable in the eyes of other people. It is simply a matter of helping [them] see that what [they] see as shameful or foolish is old stuff to you' (1946, p.396). This does not mean playing down or dismissing aspects of the client's life that are worrying or important to them. We can acknowledge the difficulty or concern without sharing their sense of anxiety or alarm. This is best done in a seamless and conversational way:

Client:	I actually think about suicide sometimes.
Therapist:	It's not uncommon for people to think like that and I've met quite a few people who have talked about it. Was it a serious consideration with you or just one of those ideas we get from time to time?
Client:	I feel as if everybody is looking at me and I start to get nervous.
Therapist:	Join the club! It can be quite tense going somewhere new for the first time. How do you deal with that?
Client:	I'm a lousy mother and I feel guilty about that. For example, I can't even remember things that happened early on, like his first school play, or sports day.
Therapist:	Quite a few parents have told me how difficult it is to remember all the things that happen in their kids' lives. So much goes on that we sometimes forget just how much we are doing as we learn to become a parent.

Exercise
What irksome aspect of your life do you occasionally tend to exaggerate in your thoughts or words? How can you normalise it by describing it in less dramatic terms, and in a way that makes it appear more 'normal'?

Reframing

To reframe is to offer a new interpretation or viewpoint for an experience. It has the effect of challenging and introducing doubt into old, unproductive beliefs. By offering a reframe the therapist demonstrates that they see the client's situation and ideas as something other than fixed, rigid conditions. In their classic work entitled *Change: Principles of Problem Formation and Problem Resolution* (1974), Watzlawick *et al.* say that reframing is: 'to change the conceptual and/or emotional setting or viewpoint…and to place it in another frame which fits the "facts" of the same concrete situation equally well or even better, and thereby changes its entire meaning.' In other words, we may not be able to change the 'facts', but we can change the client's interpretation of the facts.

Who among us has not found themselves struggling with some difficulty, unable to see a way out of it because we are caught in the trap of our own making: we only have one way of interpreting an event and that interpretation hurts or upsets us. For example, I call my friend John, he is out, so I leave a message for him to call me back. He does not call, ergo, he does not want to speak to me. I start to feel bad because this confirms what I already 'know' – John does not like me really – our 'friendship' is a sham. I only have one viewpoint (John does not want to speak to me) and that viewpoint is limiting. Left alone with these thoughts and – assuming that I am unable to come up with some other explanations on my own – I am likely to fall foul of my own circular reasoning and dig an even bigger hole for myself. (He didn't call, therefore he doesn't want to, therefore there is no point in me calling him, etc.) Unless I can find some way of breaking this pattern I am stuck.

Rubin Battino, in his book *Expectation: The Very Brief Therapy Book* (2006), says that there are two questions to ask when constructing a reframe:

> 'In what context can this experience occur that would make it more beneficial to this client?'

> 'What other meanings can be assigned to this experience that would make it beneficial?' (pp.31–32).

This illustrates that reframing is concerned with both context and meaning (or interpretation) of an event or set of circumstances.

Conversely, we have all been on the receiving end of some well-intentioned advice of the every-cloud-has-a-silver-lining variety. Such clumsy attempts to cheer someone up following an unfortunate event usually fall on unreceptive ears simply because they do not agree with what I am thinking or feeling at the time. Unless the alternative interpretation is plausible to me I am unlikely to accept it, worse, I will probably think that you just haven't heard me. The key thing that differentiates reframing from this sort of comment is that the reframe is acceptable to the client (or at least is not rejected by them) because it matches the events just as well as their original, and limiting, interpretation.

Reframing is a fundamental part of therapeutic conversations because it can help the client start to break up their rigid patterns of thinking. However, the important thing here is to understand that choice exists; we do not necessarily have to exercise it. It is therefore important to remember, if you are unfamiliar with this type of conversational gambit, that the idea here is not necessarily to get the client to visibly agree with our suggestions, or to fall on their knees in gratitude for our insightful comments. Simply showing that we do not necessarily buy into their world view, by speculating on the alternatives and then moving on, can be a powerful intervention. 'The goal of therapy is to participate in a conversation that continually loosens and opens up… In such a context, meanings are changed, thus creating more choices for change' (Anderson and Goolishan 1988, p.377).

Examples of reframes

Client: They say I am a manic depressive.
Therapist: They also say that people who have these symptoms are very creative; what are your particular talents?

Client: I never seem to make decisions, it takes me so long to make up my mind.
Therapist: So you take time to weigh things up. Don't they say there is wisdom in caution?

Client: We've been married twenty years, and we've been arguing just as long.
Therapist: I know that some couples have a naturally combative communication style.

Ideally, reframing seeks to suggest a positive intention to the problematic behaviour (creativity, rather than mood swings; combative communication style, rather than arguing), the positive function of symptoms, or their positive unintended consequences (Cooper 1995).

'Reframing strategies encourage an alternative viewpoint of experience. When a clinician says "Look at it from another perspective" the clinician is encouraging reframing. Reframing means deriving different interpretations and meanings from the same set of data' (Yapko 1992, p.172).

In therapy, as in life, choice tends to offer greater freedom than no choice. When we only have one way of looking at a situation we effectively have no choice at all. Reframing offers alternatives; meanings are changed and choice is the result.

Reframing is a constant in the therapeutic or helping relationship and can be either directly stated to the client or suggested indirectly through metaphor, examples and homework assignments. An example of the latter might be to ask a client who is locked into a one-dimensional view of someone else's behaviour to make a list of all the possible explanations they can think of.

Looking for exceptions

Even clients with the most apparently intractable difficulties have moments when the difficulty is a bit less intense, or even absent from their thinking. Nothing is constant, change is happening all the time (alright, so change is constant). Faced with adversity most of us tend to focus on the problem, often to a point where it dominates our lives. But there are exceptions: depression lifts for an hour or a day; anxiety takes a back seat when we are distracted by something and become engrossed in it; physical pain diminishes for a while and we are able to function better as a result. Since that which we focus on becomes our reality, the more we focus on the problem the more real it seems to us. Looking for exceptions – those moments when we are free of the problem or when it diminishes its hold over us – is a way to help the client start to break these thinking patterns and bring balance and a sense of control.

Identifying exceptions invites the client to examine just how significant the problem really is, and provides evidence to challenge the all-pervasive nature of the difficulties the client may be facing. In listening the solution focused helper of course acknowledges the difficulties, but at the same time listens for times when the problem is not present, or when it does not hinder the client as much as it appears to at other times.

There are always exceptions ready to be discovered and it is the helper's job to identify and draw these out. The rationale is that if a client's problem is present for 50 per cent of their time, then something else must be happening in the other 50 per cent. The practitioner should ask about what is happening in that time. How does the client manage to be problem free some of the time? Could they re-create this situation more often?

A very clear example of this happened when I was working with a school pupil who, it was claimed, had 'anger problems'. A series of angry outbursts during lessons had culminated in him threatening a teacher and being excluded. At our first session, after listening to how he understood the difficulties he was having I asked how many different lessons he had in a week. He came up with a list of twelve different subjects and about ten different teachers. It turned out that he had 'kicked off' in two different lessons in recent weeks. I was really interested in the other ten. After a few minutes discussing this with him, and asking, for example, how he managed to behave well in those other ten lessons, a picture began to emerge of a young man who was behaving acceptably for most of the school week. While recognising that his angry outbursts were a problem, they were not the whole story. By asking about exceptions he was able to start redefining himself in a more balanced way; rather than someone with 'anger problems', he was someone who occasionally lost it. What is more, since he knew how to remain in control most of the time, it might be possible to use some of this skill of remaining calm in situations where he previously had not. A more balanced and empowering starting point.

Exercise

We tend not to see what we do not believe is there. When we have a problem we are naturally problem focused when thinking about it. This exercise will help you train your mind to look for problem-free times, exceptions, as a matter of course.

Think of an everyday nuisance or problem in your life. This can be anything that irritates or bothers you. Somebody else's behaviour, some aspect of your behaviour…anything.

In considering this irritant or difficulty:

- Think of the times when it *does not* happen. Think of all the examples you can, and make a list.

- Note any times when the problem is present, but not bothering you or you are unaware of it.

- Consider what percentage of your time this problem is either actively present in your life, or you spend thinking about it (passively present).

Revisit this every day for a week. Take note of whether the list of problem-free times (exceptions) gets longer, the problem becomes less invasive or the percentage of problem-free time increases.

Externalising

When the problem is seen as being part of the client – or part of their character – it is difficult for them to deal with it effectively. Externalisation rests on the idea that however pervasive a problem is, or however much it impacts on a person's life, it is nevertheless separate from them, not part of them. In the now famous words of Michael White, 'Neither the person nor the relationship between persons is the problem. Rather the problem becomes the problem' (White and Epston 1990, p.40). This has been summarised more succinctly as 'The person is not the problem, the problem is the problem' (Freedman and Combs 1996). Karl Tomm says that externalising entails 'a linguistic separation of the distinction of the problem from the personal identity of the patient' (Tomm 1989, p.16).

By the time they turn to us for help clients have often come to believe that something about them is problematic. The problem has become 'internalised'. Diagnostic labelling is partly responsible for this. Think of the jargon we regularly use: alcoholic, depressive, schizophrenic, anxious, phobic, anorexic…the list is very long. Each time we make a label out of a set of symptoms and attach it someone they are likely to start believing that they are the same thing as their symptoms (Tomm 1989). This has the effect of defining the person in terms of their symptoms and experience. If I believe myself to be 'a depressive' or 'schizophrenic', it will be more difficult for me to marshal my resources and start to make change, than if I understand that I am someone who feels depressed from time to time (or even regularly), or someone who suffers with symptoms of schizophrenia. In order to tackle my problems I need to develop the idea that I can have influence – or agency – over them. Incidentally, diagnostic labels can also bamboozle therapists: 'While these labels can be helpful at times, the biggest problem with labelling someone as "borderline", "narcissistic" or "antisocial" is that the label doesn't automatically suggest something active that you can do as a therapist to deal with the problem.' (Gottman 1999, p.266).

The aim of externalising is to enable people to see that they and the problem are separate entities, not the same thing. This conceptual shift enables the client to combat the pernicious effect of believing the problem to be part of them. By objectifying it and giving the problem an identity which is external to them, the client is able to find new ways of escaping or managing the influence of the problem.

> Externalizing is an approach to therapy that encourages persons to objectify and, at times, to personify the problems that they experience as oppressive. In this process, the problem becomes a separate identity and thus external to the person or relationship that was ascribed as the problem. Those problems that are considered to be inherent, as well as those with relatively fixed qualities that are attributed to persons and to relationships, are rendered less fixed and less restricting. (White and Epston 1990, p.38)

In helping clients to separate themselves from the problem externalisation opens up the possibilities for them to describe themselves from a new, non-problem-saturated viewpoint, from which they can begin to perceive qualities in themselves and aspects of their lives that hitherto were obscured or denied by the pervasiveness of the problem.

The practice of externalising seeks to:

- undermine the sense of failure that may have developed in the client due to the continuation of the problem despite their attempts to fix it

- open new possibilities for clients to take action to retrieve their lives and relationships from the problem and its influence

- free people to take a lighter, more effective and less stressed approach to serious problems

- provide opportunities for discussing problems from a new perspective

- enable clients to separate from the dominant and 'problem-saturated' stories that have dominated their lives

- enable clients to identify and harness previously neglected but vital aspects of their experience.

(White and Epston 1990; Freedman and Combs 1996)

Successful externalisation stems from an attitude on the part of the therapist or helper, rather than a trick or device to be employed in certain situations (Freedman and Combs 1996). Thus, it is not something that we 'do to people' but a natural extension of the conversation in which language is chosen to help the client become aware of the separateness of between themselves and the problem; that they are not it, but in a relationship with it. Perhaps they cannot influence the problem, but they can influence the relationship; how it impacts on them and affects their lives.

Exercise

1. IDENTIFYING THE PROBLEM

Pick an adjective that describes a quality or aspect of yourself that you feel you have/experience too much, or which others criticise you for (the problem). For example 'angry', 'controlling', 'impatient', 'critical'. Respond to the following using the chosen aspect to replace 'X'.

- How did you become X?

- What typically leads to you being X?

- What does being X mean in your life and your relationships?

- What troubles you the most about being X?

- What do you do too much of because you are X?

- Consider how you feel in answering these questions. How limiting is this? What seems possible/impossible as a result of X?

- How do you feel after answering these questions? How much control do you think you have over the problem? How will this develop in the future?

Now change the subject by thinking about something else for a moment or two. For example, what did you have for breakfast?

2. EXTERNALISING THE PROBLEM

Now to give the problem a name which defines it as a separate entity. Convert the adjective 'X' into a noun, 'Y'. So for example 'controlling' becomes 'control', 'impatient' becomes 'Impatience', 'critical' becomes 'critic' (you can liven this up by converting them into entities with names like 'Fat Controller' or 'The Critical Voice'). Naming the problem in this way gives it an identity.

Respond to the following using the problem's new identity to replace 'Y'.

- How did Y manage to gain influence over your life?

- What does Y have you believing about yourself?

- In what ways does Y spoil your relationships?

- In what contexts or situations is Y most likely to take over?

- How does Y persuade you to ignore the good advice you give yourself?

- Have you noticed times when Y doesn't manage to take over?

- What is happening when you manage to keep Y at bay?

- What actions might you take as a couple that might shrink the effects of 'not listening?'

Notice the difference in the two styles of questioning. You should notice that by redefining the quality as a noun, giving it a name, and then answering the second set of questions, you began to externalise it.

- How might this be useful in dealing with the problem?

- What difference do you notice in how you feel about the problem?

- How will you interact differently with the problem in future

(adapted from Freedman and Combs 1996, pp.49–50)

Externalising questions begin to embed the idea that the client has choices, increasing their sense of control over the problem and helping them see themselves as an active agent in the course of their lives. Over time this greater sense of personal agency and the therapeutic conversations it makes possible combine in a process of personal empowerment for the client (Tomm 1989).

Scaling

Scaling is, in my opinion, one of the most influential aspects of this whole array of gizmos I am discussing here. The results of introducing the notion of degree into a conversation has practical implications which go far beyond the simplicity of the idea.

In a world that tends to deal in polar opposites and 'either–or' type of thinking it is useful to remember that few aspects of our lives are totally one thing or another. Things happen by degree or increment and we also experience them with different degrees of intensity at different times. Between the two extremes of 'happy' and 'sad', 'success' and 'failure', or 'able' and 'disabled' there are infinite shades of meaning that most of us fail to see, especially when under pressure or in distress. Scaling seeks to reintroduce the idea that breaking things down can make them more manageable. Scaling then:

- introduces the idea of incremental thinking
- makes the intangible appear tangible
- elicits 'quantitative' information for risk assessment and other purposes
- moves from the abstract to the concrete
- offers the possibility of measurement
- can demonstrate that change is already happening
- helps develop the client's strategy for working towards their goals
- demonstrates that change is happening all the time.

This can be used anywhere in the session, and in particular any time it would be useful to move from abstract or vague concepts to something more specific and measurable.

I was working with a young man who was struggling in his relationships with some of his colleagues, and they in turn found him difficult to get along with. He kept using the same term every time he spoke about an emotional response. In his vocabulary, 'stressed' seemed to mean anything from mildly irritated to extremely angry. If as they say, 'you can't measure it you can't manage it', and this man was unable to distinguish different levels of arousal, then he might be having difficulty gauging his reactions. By asking him to give a rating (scale of 1 to 10), to different aspects of his experience we developed a whole way for him to talk about his emotional reactions, and to understand the difference, for example, between a '3' and an '8'. Pretty soon he was able to distinguish between different levels of emotional arousal and name them. Whereas he had used the blanket term 'stressed' any time he felt any degree of upset, now he could identify when he was irritated, bored, frustrated or angry, and tell the difference between the different states. Management of the emotions starts with being able to recognise them and distinguish degrees of arousal (Meichenbaum 2001).

By the way, people in my workshops often ask if it important which way round the numbers are used. I tend to use 1 to equal 'no problem' and 10 to equal 'extreme problem', because that makes sense to me, but it really doesn't matter as long as you are consistent. In fact, when I have asked some clients to rate a particularly intrusive symptom on a scale of 1 to 10, they have replied with a '1' or a '2', even though they have spent the previous half hour explaining all the difficulties associated with the symptom. On my scale I would have expected a high number, so I assume that their scale works the other way round. When this happens I check with them and then go with their method.

Neither does it have to always be numbers; I have used the colour spectrum with a painter, with different colours as gradations, and musical scales with a musician.

Finally, when scaling the numbers are relative only to the client's experience and mean nothing outside that context. Scaling is a way of understanding how the client views their experience, of providing a way of speaking about that experience, and of framing to conversation so that it can lead to small achievable goals. It can also be used to assess levels of motivation.

Exercise

Practise scaling as often as you reasonably can and it will soon become a habit. For example, on a scale of 1 to 10, how hungry are you now? If 10 is ravenous, where you actually have to eat, ask yourself:

- Where am I now (number)?

- At what point on the scale do I start to feel slightly hungry but do not want to eat?

- At what point on the scale do I get so hungry that it becomes imperative that I eat?

You can practise this on any aspect of your life, particularly with vague or abstract concepts like stress, tolerance, fatigue, anger, etc. So, for example, if your 'stress scale' tells you that the level of stress you experience on holiday is 2, and an unacceptable level of work stress is for you, say, 6, what would you say is an acceptable level of stress at work? And while you are at it, name one thing that you could do to reduce your level of work stress by one point.

Metaphor

Metaphor is symbolic language essential to how we think, communicate and learn, so it is also a powerful and effective device for use in therapy

(Mills and Crowley 1986). Both in and out of therapy 'Metaphors have the power to change attitudes – swiftly, without fuss and often permanently' (Haden Elgin 1999, p.87). It is said that the ability to think conceptually is one of the distinguishing characteristics of our species. Our thought processes are largely metaphorical (Lakoff and Johnson 1980), and being human means we can use mental imagery as no other animal can (Glucksberg 2001; Pinker 1997). Christopher Booker (2004) says that the real significance of our capacity to imagine stories lies in the fact that they emerge from a part of the mind that is beyond our conscious control, so to a great degree they are products of the unconscious. Lakoff and Johnson (1980) go further and say that metaphor unites the imagination with reason and so it can be seen as 'imaginative reality'.

People everywhere make use of stories to convey meaning in a way that is deeper and richer than simply reporting a string of facts or series of events. Parables, teaching tales, fairy stories, poetry, literature and art speak a symbolic language that helps us both express ourselves and grasp concepts that cannot be easily communicated any other way (Battino and South 1999; Chaika 2000).

Think for a moment about the book you are reading, far more than simply a bundle of paper sheets used to display printed text, the notion of 'book' is also a metaphor with almost limitless meanings. Life is an open book, we all have our own unique story and, as authors of our own lives we have several options, as in, when we want to move on, we can always turn the page; we know not to judge a book by its cover, yet we often do, even repeating the mistake in successive chapters of our lives, but we may continue to hope we'll find a happy ending.

Metaphor is powerful and effective in communication and therapy because it bypasses the normal process that we apply when we are taking in new information. The Greek root of the word means to carry over or transfer, and stories, anecdotes, proverbs and many other metaphorical forms contain within them far more meaning than the words themselves convey. We can therefore think of stories and metaphors as vehicles that contain more meaning than is apparent at first glance. Parables, proverbs and nursery rhymes, among others, manage, in a few words, to convey meaning which is both deep and rich and which is understood at both conscious and unconscious levels.

When we hear a metaphor we do not critically examine it, and it slips past the conscious editor we all carry around with us. Consider the following for example:

Client: I have so many problems it often seems as if I'm wasting my
              time trying to hold down a job.

Helper: Well, I realise it must be difficult. Work means that you earn
              a living and it also gives you an opportunity to leave the
              house and meet people.

Compared with:

Client: I have so many problems it often seems as if I'm wasting my
              time trying to hold down a job.

Helper: It must be difficult. I'm struck by how you manage it despite
              the challenge, going out each day to see what the world has
              to offer. How do you remain on top of things?

In the first scenario the helper acknowledges that he/she has heard
the client, then offers some reasonable reasons as reassurance. There is
nothing inaccurate in the helper's reply, but there is plenty for the client to
reject and even feel pressured by. In the second example the response also
acknowledges the client's difficulties, and then uses metaphor – contrast
this with the rather literal language in the first example – to weave a
different narrative. Not only is this potentially inspiring and uplifting
because it reframes the client's struggle as a series of mini triumphs each
day ('managing' the difficulties, facing the 'challenge', seeing what 'the
world has to offer'), it also engages the client in a way they are less likely
to reject or contradict.

Transforming meaning

In the example above the helper gently starts to transform the meaning
of the client's situation. In reframing the narrative 'many problems' and
'waste of time' through metaphor it is unlikely that the client would feel
that they are being in any way contradicted or disagreed with. Contrast
the helper's reframing with the sort of response a friend or family member
might use. We often try to cheer people up by providing evidence that,
in effect, sets out to contradict them, for example by reminding them
of all the good things in their life when they are complaining of some
unhappiness.

If, in response to the client's description of their situation above,
they are reminded that they have things to be thankful for, however
well intended the remarks, far from persuading them to change their

view it is more likely to confirm their feeling of being misunderstood. Information provided as a metaphor, however, can be far more engaging and compelling. Stories engage the mind, and to some extent distract us, and the metaphorical meaning can be taken in at an unconscious level. This makes learning and the transformation of ideas relatively effortless and more effective (Battino and South 1999).

Let's take the everyday example 'Every cloud has a silver lining', or 'Life is a journey' (I probably wouldn't use either by the way, they are too hackneyed and unoriginal to sound as if I care, but they illustrate my point). The 'every cloud' metaphor captures the idea that good things can come out of bad. If I say to someone who has just had a bad experience that it'll probably turn out alright and they might even learn from the experience, while this might be a reasonable assumption, the client can consciously challenge these statements and might feel that I haven't understood because I am offering information that does not match where they are right now, in difficulty and feeling bad about it. 'Every cloud...' on the other hand, carries with it several suggestions (clouds pass, gloomy weather is eventually always followed by fine weather, 'silver' might be discovered in unexpected places, etc.).

There is a second way that helpers can use the transformational power of metaphor. Clients' stories provide an instant source of material that can be subtly repackaged (reframed) and delivered back to them. Clients of course use metaphor to describe their experience. The helper can listen for this and extend or transform the metaphor, thus offering an extended or transformed meaning of the situation the client describes.

I was once speaking to a couple about their infertility problems. IVF had not been successful, and they were now trying to come to terms with this. It had been suggested that they consider 'alternatives', and both friends and professionals had been free in offering suggestions such as fostering and adoption. These well-intentioned attempts had only increased the couple's sense of isolation and hopelessness. The woman, in particular, was experiencing, in her words, a 'sense of finality' after the many arduous months spent on the emotional roller-coaster of repeated attempts at IVF.

When I asked her about the term she had used, to say more about this 'sense of finality', she looked up at me and said 'I've come to a brick wall, there is no way past it.' I said, 'Sounds pretty final' (acknowledging her view). Then asked 'Can you tell me about that wall?' She replied that there was no way round it or over it, then added 'Well, I'd need a bloody long ladder.' After a short pause I asked 'And…?' She replied, '…and I suppose, if I eventually got to the top, I might be able to see what lay beyond.'

This spoke volumes. In one short sentence she was telling me what she had been saying to the well-meaning friends and helpers for weeks: 'This is not the time, there might eventually come a time when I can recognise that there are other options, but not now.' Only after a long climb might she be able to acknowledge that something lay beyond the 'brick wall' of her current situation.

We continued our conversation. There was no more need to discuss the hopelessness. She had in effect said that she needed time. She knew there was a future, but she was unable to consider it yet. So we talked about how they, the couple, might start to heal, and they spoke about grieving, and how they could support each other. There was more, of course, but in this instance, taking her metaphor of the wall, and talking about the metaphor (rather than talking directly about what it represented), provided a transformative moment in the session.

The power of metaphor is often missed by helpers, and even by some therapists. It is powerful because it is so descriptive and, as the examples here suggest, it provides a unique way of helping others learn and understand. Every culture in the world uses metaphor and it is so central to how we communicate, learn and change, that it might justly be thought of as mankind's original therapy.

Exercise

- Think of something you would like to change in your life, then create three metaphors that you might use to describe it (if you have trouble doing this start with 'It's like…'): e.g. 'Meal times in our house are like a battleground', or 'He goes deaf when I raise the question of money.'

- Staying with the metaphor in each case, describe what is needed to do to correct it, e.g. peace, communicating with a deaf person.

- Imagine yourself using the corrective action: e.g. calling a truce, using sign language.

- How can you harness your metaphorical solutions? For example, how might you alter your behaviour to move towards a solution of the problem?

The goal of this exercise is to help you become more aware of the metaphors you use, and to enable you to consciously use them in the construction of solutions. You may also start to recognise links with areas of competence in your life where you had not previously seen them.

Questions

Questions are fundamental to SFBT. So important, in fact, that I have given them a chapter to themselves (Chapter 8). Questions are both the reasons people get into difficulty with their lives and simultaneously the route away from problems and towards solutions. A story told to me by Michael Yapko some years ago makes this distinction clearer. Michael lives in California and the region was struck by the Loma Prieta earthquake in 1989. Sadly, people died and there was widespread damage to property. Picture two neighbours in a street destroyed by the 'quake, as they survey what is left of their homes. The first, George, keeps asking himself 'Why me?', the second, Marcus, asks a different question, 'What shall I do about it?' We do not know how George and Marcus fared in the aftermath of the earthquake, but we can hazard a guess at their respective levels of motivation.

Questions call for actions but, as this example shows, not all questions are equal and some engage us in action that keeps us stuck, while others get us moving or thinking differently. The questions we ask, internal as above or external when a helper asks a question of a client, determine the direction we move in. Solution focused practitioners pay a lot of attention to the questions they ask and the outcomes they hope to instigate in asking them.

Presuppositions

In linguistic terms, which is what I am discussing here, presuppositions underpin many statements or questions and are designed to function as interventions in themselves. Presuppositions are not openly stated; they are embedded in the language we use and work discreetly and, usually, unconsciously. In life our presuppositions are what guide us in many situations ('John is always late so John will be late today; Respectable people have a regular job so if I am out of work I become less respectable.'). Our clients' untested negative presuppositions often cause them grief or contribute to their difficulties. In SFBT we actively use positive presuppositions ('When you no longer need to see a therapist'; 'What will be different after the miracle', etc).

The therapist uses future-oriented phrases when talking about the improvements the client wants. By saying to a client, 'How will it be when you are (happy) again?' as well as presupposing success we are also asking the person to look into the future and envision the problem solved, something which, very often, they will not have done before.

We are all familiar with the sort of presuppositional question which goes something like, 'When did you stop beating your wife?' where there is no answer which does not constitute an admission of guilt. Therapeutic presuppositions work the other way round by directing clients to answers that promote the positive. 'How did you bring about the improvement?' presupposes that the client has some control in their condition while underscoring that there has been improvement. A presuppositional statement might be 'What positive things have happened to you since we last met?'

SFBT uses a high degree of presupposition. Helpers and therapists consistently demonstrate in their language that they assume a positive outcome is inevitable. We use words like 'will', 'when' and 'yet' when speaking about clients' aims and goals (O'Hanlon and Weiner-Davis 1989). Presupposing success and positive improvement are built into the founding question of the SF approach, 'How do we construct solutions?', and others (see Chapter 4), guide our thinking.

Responding with presuppositions

Client: I'm really bad at choosing my partners, I always end up with abusive people.

Therapist: So you've had some bad experiences and you'd like to choose more wisely in future?

Client: I can never hold down a job.

Therapist: Based on experience, you say you've changed jobs a lot. What sort of job would you like to be doing when one becomes more permanent?

Client: I'm a hopeless case. I'll probably need to see you for years.

Therapist: I do brief therapy, most people see me for between three to six sessions. That's enough for most people to make me redundant.

General to specific

One of the ways that SFBT practitioners help clients think more critically about their situation is by listening for generalisations and coaxing the client to become more specific. We are all familiar with the joke 'I've told you a million times, don't exaggerate.' Clients will often make sweeping generalisations such as 'Men can't be trusted', or 'I didn't sleep a wink last night.' While it is important not to deny the client's view of things, such statements can be gently and consistently challenged to great effect. For instance, in the second example above we might ask probing questions to establish that, in fact, the client did sleep for several hours, but that their sleep was intermittent. The process of challenging will start to change negative beliefs held by the client, and introduce a more realistic view which is less 'all or nothing'.

Client: I have been anxious since birth.

Therapist: You can remember that far back?

Client: No, my doctor told me so.

Therapist: Has your doctor known you since you were a baby?

Client: Well, no.

Therapist: So, how do you know you have been anxious since birth?

Client: My mother told me, she always said that I was an anxious child.

Therapist: And how about you, what recollections do you have about being anxious?

Client: Well, it really became noticeable when I started the job I'm in now.

Therapist: And how long have you been in this job?

Client: About five years.

Therapist: So, from your experience, you have had these symptoms of anxiety for five years or so.

Client: Yes.

Tackling a problem that is five years old seems much less daunting than taking on something that is 'lifelong', wouldn't you say? I must reiterate, the idea here is not to deny the client's experience. The aim is to help the client think in a more precise way, when their habitual way of thinking –

as far as we can tell from the language – is upholding a limiting belief, and one that is genuinely open to question. (How many babies are diagnosed with anxiety-related problems?)

Language should have a positive orientation

When working with clients, therapists should always ensure that their language is progressively oriented, thus creating an expectation that positive change is possible and even likely. The therapist's language shapes the course of therapy during and after the session, and something as simple as a change of verb tense can create a sense of accomplishment, anticipation or completion. By subtly shifting from 'when you are depressed' to 'when you were depressed', and then 'when you used to be depressed', the perceptions of a person's depression can begin to alter.

In any conversation with those we support we would of course start by matching the client's language, and then start to 'channel the meanings for those words in a useful direction.' (O'Hanlon and Weiner-Davis 1989). The aim here is to move the client to a less limiting or pathological meanings to more normal descriptions. So for example, with someone who complains of a 'drink problem', the helper might start referring to their 'complaint about drink' or the 'times when they drink', because these sound less onerous and more amenable to change than a 'drink problem'. (You can see this in action in the Brenda session transcript in the Appendix.)

By using language with a positive orientation I am not suggesting an annoyingly permanent, sunny and optimistic disposition more popularly called 'positive thinking.' I am using the term to mean future oriented and leading to where the client would want to go. This is outlined in the first few points of Chapter 4:

- Clients have strengths and resources.
- The relationship between therapist and client has therapeutic value.
- Change happens all the time.
- Small change will generate larger change.
- Rapid change is possible.
- The focus is on the present and the future.
- Well-formed goals are achievable.

We can use language to initiate and bring about changes. By gradually beginning to introduce different verbal patterns into the conversation we can begin to change the client's perception, and therefore their experience, of their problem. We can do this in many ways, conversationally and without effort. However, just as the way we speak to our clients has the potential for therapeutic change, it can also have negative effects by reinforcing negative beliefs, confirming symptoms and even implanting false ideas if not used with care.

I have given an overview and some examples of the more widely used devices that are available to therapists and helpers. These are not restricted to SFBT – most therapists use reframing and normalising, for example, and externalising is finding its way into all sorts of settings like mediation and behaviour management – but SF practitioners use them all the time and see them as therapeutic in and of themselves.

Other authors have dealt with this in greater detail, and if you wish to study this aspect further two essential books are *Ericksonian Approaches* (Battino and South 1999) and O'Hanlon and Beadle's *A Field Guide to Possibility Land* (1994). As a primer, and an eminently readable introduction to the elements of therapeutic communication *The Language of Change* by Paul Watzlawick (1978) is not to be missed. While you do not need to read so extensively to be proficient or even excellent at using the skills of SFBT, serious students should acquaint themselves with the reading, and in addition anything by or about the grandfather of the field, Dr Milton Erickson, will open up a whole new avenue of exploration in the language of therapy.

CHAPTER 8

Questions Are Keys

In an earlier section I described the fundamental importance of the creative use of questions. Therapy will be more efficient and more effective when we use well formed questions. Conversely, poor questions will get poor results and may even hold up therapy or reinforce a client's limiting perceptions.

> Questions, of course, are an important communication element of all models of therapy. Therapists use questions often with all approaches, especially while taking history, checking in at the beginning of a session, or finding out how a homework assignment went. SFBT therapists, however, make questions the *primary* communication tool, and as such they are an overarching intervention. SFBT therapists tend to make no interpretations, and rarely make direct challenges or confrontations to a client. (de Shazer *et al.* 2007, pp.4–5)

Therapeutic questions have been likened to 'treasure hidden in broad daylight' (Goldberg 1998), as the simplest of questions can trigger profound change or insight. They do far more than gather information and in therapy, as in life, the right question can open our perceptions and start us on a road to discovery, healing, growth and change. When we take time to consider how we speak, think and listen, we quickly realise that questioning is one of the most essential tools we have in language.

They are the basis on which helping and therapy are conducted, yet how to construct questions and use them skilfully is one of the least studied aspects during the training of therapists, for whom language is a primary tool. This is not limited to therapy of course, our daily lives are founded on questions asked and answered (or not), and the question is probably our most common form of linguistic exchange. For all this, few of us ever study questions, preferring the habits we grew up with and developed throughout our lives. Effective enough for most of us, to be sure, but haphazard in the extreme and completely inadequate when it comes to therapeutic communication of any kind.

Karl Tomm, in a series of seminal papers on the use of questions in family therapy, explores the range of effects that questions can have:

> I have become fascinated with the variety of effects a therapist can have on individual clients or families during the course of a clinical interview. In a conventional session, most of the therapist's questions ostensibly are designed to help him or her formulate an assessment. The questions themselves are not usually regarded as interventions to help clients. Yet, many questions do have therapeutic effects on family members (directly) through the implications of the questions and/or (indirectly) through the verbal and non-verbal responses of family members to them. At the same time, however, some of the therapist's questions can be counter-therapeutic. (1987, p.172)

Carefully crafted questions used skilfully do far more than just elicit information from the client, and I have known cases where a single question has been all that is necessary to enable the client to kick-start a process of change in their lives. In her book *The Art of the Question* (1998), Marilee Goldberg sets the scene with 'the whole domain of question asking, both internal and external, represents a gold mine of interventions, strategies and ways of thinking about therapy itself that can enhance both its effectiveness and its efficiency' (p.4). Meichenbaum sums this up:

> Of all the assessment tools available, the most valuable is the clinical interview and the most important therapeutic skill is the art of questioning. The questions that therapists pose to patients are often more important than the answers patients offer or the advice that therapists give. The questions that therapists pose help patients to co-construct new 'life stories' as well as providing (them) with a cognitive model for a style of thinking. (2001, p.147).

So questions should not be used willy-nilly because they can harm as well as help, but used thoughtfully the range of purposes to which questions can be put is almost limitless, and the effects can be carried beyond the session for, as Tomm (1987) says, clients often 'carry questions home' and continue to work on them on their own. Questions function as a bridge between problem and solution, enabling the client to formulate new choices and courses of action that will lead towards self-healing (Goldberg 1998; O'Hanlon and Weiner-Davis 1989; Tomm 1987). The questions the helper chooses to ask determine not only the direction of the session but the entire course of the therapy.

As an example, think of a client who says 'My life is a total failure'. The therapist can respond in a number of ways and each will take the conversation in a different direction. He or she might say 'Tell me more', or 'What makes you think that?', or even 'How have you managed so well so far?' Let's look at how these three responses influence the course of the conversation.

'Tell me more'

This simple statement does a number of things. It acknowledges what the client has said without contradicting it, and asks for more information. It is a safe, rather unimaginative question, the stuff of many therapy sessions, which encourages the client to give more information and so focus on the problem. The next stage of a session where this question is used is fairly predictable as the client is invited to continue in the same vein, reifying the abstract statement about life into something concrete and immovable.

'What makes you think that?'

This also acknowledges that the therapist has heard the client, but from then on it does something different: it asks for evidence. In effect it says, 'I have heard what you said, and I want to understand how you arrived at that conclusion.' There is the hint of a challenge in this. The client has to do some work. They are being asked, compassionately of course, to explain what led them to this all-encompassing belief. Nobody's life is a total failure and although we all use generalisations like this, here the client actually appears to take this self-limiting belief as fact. They are unable to apply critical thinking or to mitigate this damning message of hopelessness. In using this question the helper does not openly challenge or contradict the client, but neither does he or she go along with it unquestioningly as the client seems to be doing. Since the client is not questioning this self-limiting belief, the therapist lightly introduces the idea that it might usefully be questioned.

'How have you managed so well so far?'

Here we have a truly solution focused question. Once again, the client's original statement is implicitly acknowledged, and then it takes off in a different direction by also suggesting, in the view of the therapist, that the client has 'managed well'. To answer this question the client will have to start looking for the resources that have enabled them to cope and continue to function.

All three of these responses are supportive in that they affirm the client's original statement. From there though each will take the conversation in an entirely different direction.

These are just examples and a creative therapist or helper will develop their own style of questions. I have often heard trainees say how unsure they are about being able to develop this skill. The right sort of creativity comes with practice, and it also helps, as with any creative process, to 'let go' of one's inhibitions and self-doubt. As we learn something new – singing, playing a musical instrument, writing – although it may initially need conscious effort we gradually develop a facility which means we can work more intuitively.

People who are new to this sometimes ask how clients respond to these unusual questions. I usually give two answers to this. The first responds to what I believe underlies the question: won't my clients find it strange if I ask things which take me outside my comfort zone? So response number one is, What if they do? Don't clients seek help in order to do something different, to learn something that'll take them towards more satisfactory ways of living? I would say I have an obligation to develop my questioning skills and remain creative in using them if I am going to be any use to my clients. Answer number two is that clients quickly get used to being asked unusual or unexpected questions, in fact they come to expect it.

Curiosity and stupidity

Curiosity is one of the cornerstones of SF practice and it prompts constant questions. One of the great attributes of working in a solution focused way is that it requires the helper or therapist to be extremely *curious*. In order to be curious, of course, we have to be interested, and interest keeps us focused on what we are doing and enthusiastic. This enthusiasm makes us eager to learn more about our client, what they are saying, how they are managing, the resources they have and generally, well, to be curious about everything.

And curiosity generates questions. These are not questions to show how wise, deep or clever the therapist is, they are questions to help understand the client's view of their world, and to help them begin to see, for example, how some of their thinking, or the view they have of events, may be having a limiting effect on them.

All questions are thought-provoking, some more than others. Though some are strange, they do not have to be weird or complicated. Simplicity is one of the hallmarks of SFBT and SF questions are frequently rather banal and might even appear stupid (McKergow and Korman 2009). Clients go along with this without complaining. I have often been told things like 'No one has ever asked me that before,' but never 'That's a silly question and I won't answer it' (though clients do sometimes struggle with *how* to answer questions). Harry Stack Sullivan, in his book on the psychiatric interview, said:

> I do not believe that I have ever had an interview (with a patient) in twenty five years in which the person to whom I was talking was not annoyed during the early part of the interview by my asking stupid questions... A patient tells me the obvious and I wonder what he means, and ask further questions. But after the first half-hour or so, he begins to see that there is reasonable uncertainty as to what he meant. (1970, p.7)

Uncertainty, as we know, is the stuff of possibilities, and possibilities is what SFBT is all about.

Question asking and critical thinking

Clients and service users are often suffering from, or having their suffering compounded by, impoverished patterns of thinking. By impoverished I mean cognitive habits which are in some way limiting so that they are unable to think their way out of their difficulties and transform their thoughts into actions if necessary. The better able a client is to apply critical thinking skills to themselves and their situation the better equipped they are to deal with life successfully (Goldberg 1998; Yapko 1999). Psychological well-being depends in large part on being able to think our way out of problems, to balance negative attributions with positive, to question our ruminations and cogitations, to reality check ourselves and our experience, and to distinguish between abstract generalisations and concrete ends. In other words, to think critically. The willingness and ability to do this, says Keeley, rests on three interrelated aspects:

1. an awareness of useful questions to ask when presented with new information

2. the skills to answer those questions

3. a set of attitudes and dispositions that encourage us to want to ask useful questions in a fair-minded way.

These attitudes comprise things like curiosity and wanting to question oneself, openness and honesty, persistence and high frustration tolerance, intellectual humility and ambiguity (Keeley 1995, p.11–12).

Reviewing Keeley's list, Goldberg concludes by saying, 'Actually, such a list makes one wonder (if) this idealized critical thinker would end up in therapy at all' (1998, p.17). This underlines the point I wish to make here. Since clients frequently are victims of their own lack of critical thinking, and this in turn is causing or contributing to their difficulties, then part of the job of the helper or therapist must be to ask the questions they are failing to ask themselves, and in turn to help them learn more productive thinking habits. Many of the questions used in SFBT are designed to do this.

Questions are interventions

Questions are, of course, a means by which to elicit information from others, but they do far more. Using them as a device to find things out about another person and their lives, we can overlook that the style and content of the questions we use – as well as the way in which they are delivered – say a lot about us, our expectations and beliefs. And it doesn't end there. How attentively we listen and the style and detail of our response continually relays information about the enquirer to the respondent; we shape the interaction in ways we often overlook.

Solution focused helpers almost invariably use questions that are about the present or focused on the future. This reflects one of the central ideas of the approach, that solutions will be found in the present or the future, by focusing on something in the client's life that is already working, or on their goals and aspirations, in other words, on what they would like to have happen in their lives.

Focusing on the past is a perfectly valid activity in some circumstances, but it doesn't play any part in a solution focused intervention, beyond acknowledging how the client got to where they are now. Hearing the story our client tells us can be a powerful rapport-builder and naturally some information about the past is important, but the bits the client will see as important may not have much therapeutic value. If they did, the client, in focusing on them, would already have done their own therapy! A solution focused practitioner will listen to the history with a 'third ear',[1] mining the narrative for information on resilience, success and survival, and so using an essentially problem focused narrative in a solution focused way, to provide examples of resources and success which the client almost always misses.[2]

Client: We have been living together for six years, and during that time he has never lifted a finger to help with the children. The first was born just after we moved in together, the next one less than two years later. I've been so busy with the children... always tired...looking after the house... I don't expect it to be plain sailing, but I could use some help. He tells me he loves me and always compliments me on our home and all the things I do... But those are just words aren't they? It is impossible to believe that he'll ever change, help me so that I can get some rest, maybe even a lie-in on a Sunday.

Therapist: It can be really tough, those first few years with children, and you have had two so close together. So the first one must

---

1   Psychiatrist W. L. Tonge describes listening with the third ear as 'fundamentally a perceiving what is not said.' I would enlarge on this by saying that in listening attentively we are looking for things that the client *has not noticed*, whether said or not (Tonge 1967, p.16).

2   Some of the critics of SFBT misunderstand this to mean that we do not listen to or validate our clients' histories. This is incorrect. Like any therapist, SFBT practitioners will listen attentively to their clients' narratives and respond appropriately with acknowledgment, compassion and the time needed for the client to feel understood and supported. However, we also listen for resources, strengths and other 'nuggets' that we can weave back into the conversation. Being solution focused does not mean that we neglect the past of the client, we just don't expect to find the solution there, or spend time constantly re-examining it.

have been two when the second was born, what a challenge that must have been.

I'm struck, though, by the way you have managed so well. Many couples go through some rough water when children first arrive, it can be a real challenge to the relationship. You two seem to have remained a loving couple despite all these challenges. I'm wondering how you have done that? And also what keeps your relationship buoyant and loving?

The therapist first normalises and acknowledges the client's situation, then asks questions which are deliberately general, but which will tend towards resourcefulness and may provide elements of skill and creativity that the client has missed. The therapist chooses to focus on the elements that present possibilities. 'Rough water' and 'buoyant' reflect the 'plain sailing' metaphor, and simultaneously reframe the situation as one of, if you like, good seamanship rather than a relationship that is sinking.

Future-oriented questions

People in crisis are usually so preoccupied with their difficulties and the perceived causes that, in effect, they are unable to see the future as being any different. We all make predictions based on past experience and in some cases this makes sound sense, but not in all cases. In fact, there are very few situations where the past is a reliable indicator of what will happen in the future.

The process of making predictions based on the past is, for many people, habitual, pernicious and limiting. As psychologist Dr Michael Yapko says when writing about depression, 'Projections are characteristically negative, self-limiting, repetitive, self-endangering and self-devaluing' (1992, p.80). This habit does not only apply to people with symptoms of depression, we all do it to some extent and some of our clients are particularly good at it. Individuals and families can get themselves trapped in a self-reinforcing cycle which they find difficult to break. In the words of Karl Tomm 'they remain impoverished with respect to future alternatives and choices' (1987, p. 172). By purposefully asking a series of well-constructed future-oriented questions the therapist or helper can disrupt the patterns of negativity and erroneous predictions and trigger a process whereby the clients start to create more of a future for themselves.

As well as asking about the future, questions should also presuppose that change is possible and that action or movement is inevitable. Change is of course inevitable as it is happening all the time; nothing is constant or static, it is just a question of making sure that the client begins to notice positive change, however small, rather than focusing endlessly on the negative aspects. If things can get worse they must inevitably get better, even if only briefly. And change is also about action and movement.

Finally, as well as developing an unextinguishable curiosity, SF practitioners are also enthusiastic about what they are doing. Done well this enthusiasm is infectious and the client will pick up on it too.

The Miracle Question

And so we come to the Miracle Question, one of the most powerful interventions there can be when used properly, yet possibly one of the most misunderstood aspects of SFBT. I'll deal with what the Miracle Question is before briefly explaining why I think it is so often misunderstood and the limiting consequences of this.

The origins of the Miracle Question are beginning to pass into mythology, and there are several versions of how it came into being. Steve de Shazer paid tribute to an earlier giant of the field by saying that the Miracle Question was an adaptation of Milton Erickson's crystal ball technique – in which the client is invited to 'look into a crystal ball' to a time when the problem has been solved, and then to look backward from the future and explain how the solution had come about. The version I prefer is that the Miracle Question was invented when one of the founders of SFBT, Insoo Kim Berg, was struggling with 'a very tired, depressed, suicidal mother' who had a background of family dysfunction and seemingly intractable problems. When asked what she needed from the session she responded with 'I am not sure that anything can be done about my life. I don't mean to be rude but I'm not even sure why I am talking to you because I am not sure if anything can be done.' Then she added, 'Unless you have a miracle.' Like a good SFBT therapist Insoo simply picked up on this and asked gently, 'Well, suppose there was a miracle, what would be different for you?' As she answered, the mother sat up, became brighter and listed all the things that would be going well and how she and her alcoholic husband would be interacting differently (Berg and Dolan 2001, p.6).

This apparently simple question was borne out of a moment of desperation and proved to be a turning point in the session. The Miracle Question has subsequently been refined over the years. Insoo Kim Berg described it as:

> Suppose a miracle happens overnight, tonight, when you go to bed. And all the problems that brought you here to talk to me today are gone. Disappeared. But because this happens while you were sleeping, you have no idea that there was a miracle during the night. The problem is all gone, all solved. So when you are slowly waking up, coming out of your sleep, what might be the first, small clue that will make you think, 'Oh my gosh. There must have been a miracle during the night. The problem is all gone? (Yalom 2003)

The version of the Miracle Question I use is:

> This might seem like a strange question, but let's see where it takes us. Imagine that tonight, while you are asleep, a miracle happens. When you wake up, the problem that brought you here has gone. Because you were asleep, you will not know that the miracle has happened, but somehow you know that the problem has gone. How will you know? What will tell you it has gone? What will be different?

Using the Miracle Question

Though the wording may vary a little, I encourage practitioners to start by learning and using the wording exactly as it is above (either version). The reason for this is that I have noticed, in my workshops, that even a subtle shift in the words used can change the question so that it becomes less effective. The question invites the client to imagine a post-problem situation, and in order to do this they need to step out of the mindset they are currently in and, in effect, to visualise how things might be if the problem has gone. The question appears simple, but behind this apparent simplicity lie a wealth of opportunities for both the client and the helper. Once the client has engaged with the question the therapist needs to be extremely attentive and sensitive to all aspects of the client's response.

The idea is to invite the client to step into a future which is problem free. In effect this is a mini-visualisation process – the client 'goes somewhere else' – and in order to respond they must immerse themselves in their imagination. From this standpoint they can describe how they will be when the problem has gone. Further questioning enables them to develop their problem-free imagery and, the more detailed and developed the picture they describe, the easier it will be for them to start on a path of change. As with any new skill, the skills of SFBT improve with practice. Experienced practitioners thus make the Miracle Question look effortless, and this can conceal the richness and depth of the intervention. My advice is to practise the Miracle Question, and also to practise listening attentively to the client's response in order to help them develop their vision of how life post-problem would be.

Different authors attribute a wide variety of purposes to the Miracle Question, among them:

- as a catalyst for change (envisioned future) (O'Hanlon and Weiner-Davis 1989)

- to make a future time of change and health more real (Berg and Miller 1992)

- to prepare for exceptions

- to create a virtual miracle and an emotional experience

- to create a progressive story (de Shazer et al. 2007)

- to help clients identify solutions and elicit goals (O'Connell and Palmer 2003)

- to gain and maintain rapport and cooperation

- to gain insight into the client's world view

- to establish well-formed treatment goals (Miller, Hubble and Duncan 1996).

I agree with all these, and it does more besides. The reason that I preface the Miracle Question with 'This might seem like a strange question' is that it is a strange question. Clients of therapists and others in the helping professions are not used to hearing such strange questions, they are more used to talking about the past. Left to their own devices they would probably continue to do so. Asking a question about the future, and a bizarre and hypothetical one at that, suggests that more strange things are happening in therapy. SFBT practitioners actually want their clients to be surprised, and to expect the unexpected. In fact, we actually ask them to go out and look around for the unexpected (more on that later). So the Miracle Question, as well as doing all of the above, sets the scene for change by saying, in effect 'Yes, this is a strange question and who knows what'll happen next?'

An example of the Miracle Question in action

Therapist: (*after initial introductions and having listened to the client's description of the problem*) This might seem like a strange question, but let's see where it takes us. Imagine that tonight, while you are asleep, a miracle happens. When you wake up, the problem that brought you here has gone. Because you were asleep, you will not know that the miracle has happened, but somehow you will know that the problem has gone. How will you know? What will tell you it has gone? What will be different?

Client: I wake up and I'd just know.

Therapist: Yes, you'd know, *how* would you know? What would tell you that the problem has gone?

Client: Well, the first thing is that I'm feeling rested, as if I've had a good night's sleep.

Therapist: Uh huh. How does that feel?

Client: As if I can get up and face the world.

Therapist: And what tells you that. I mean, on waking, how do you know that you feel like that?

Client: My head is clearer. I'm not thinking about (the problem) as soon as I wake up. I'll be looking forward to getting up and getting on.

Therapist: And what does that mean? What will you be *doing* when you are getting up and getting on? (Looking for specific courses of action or behaviour)

Client: The first thing is I'll be hungry, looking forward to breakfast.

Therapist: What else?

Client: I'll be planning something, seeing friends rather than sitting at home all day.

Therapist: And, what else?

Client: Looking through my address book, deciding on who to call.

Therapist: (*summarising*) So you'd wake up, clear-headed, looking forward to your day, hungry and ready for breakfast, and while you're eating your breakfast you'd be planning who to call so you could get out and be socially interactive.

Client: Yes, that's it, I'd be looking forward to something.

Therapist: Anything else?

Etc.

Miracles may not be so simple

Simple though it appears the Miracle Question requires skill and confidence when using it. This is acknowledged by de Shazer *et al*.:

> To those inexperienced with or uninitiated to the subtleties of therapeutic communication, it would seem that the process of asking the Miracle Question effectively and then making practical therapeutic use of the clients' responses would be quite a simple proposition. As most people quickly discover, this is usually not the case. (2007, p.38)

This question is intended to provide a shift in client's thinking, and for this to happen there must also be a shift in the way the therapist thinks. For a client, mired in the problem and used to talking about it in a problem focused way, it is difficult to step out of the mindset that goes with their difficulties and preoccupations with the present. Responding to a question that asks them to put themselves in the future (after the miracle), requires a mental gymnastic that neither they, nor helpers or therapists, in general, are used to doing. Think about this for a moment. How often, when considering a problem in your own life, do you think 'I wonder how it would be if, when I wake up tomorrow, this problem has gone? How will I know? What will tell me the problem has gone?'

As an exercise, take a few minutes to reflect on this, notice what comes into your mind, how easy it is to avoid answering or to be distracted from the core of the question by obstructive or irrelevant ideas.

The helper must be extremely attentive to a number of things simultaneously when asking the Miracle Question:

1. Scene setting: *'This might seem like a strange question, but let's see where it takes us. Imagine that tonight, while you are asleep, a miracle happens.'* Inviting the client to participate, acknowledging that it requires a leap of faith (trust me with this strange question), presupposition, that it will lead somewhere ('let's see where it takes us'), asking the client to imagine ('while you are asleep').

2. Anticipation: *'When you wake up, the problem that brought you here has gone. Because you were asleep, you will not know that the miracle has happened, but somehow you know that the problem has gone.'* Asking the client to imagine a time in the future when they will be problem free. Note the switch to the present or future tense (*'you know... the problem has gone'*). The therapist's language must follow this shift when asking about what the client notices.

3. Evidence: *'How will you know? What will tell you it has gone? What will be different?'* The client and the helper go on a collaborative search for indicators that the problem has disappeared. The important part here is not that the problem has gone, but that the client can convincingly imagine and describe how it would be to be problem free. They should be able to do this in the present tense, or at least in the future. Both of these are more affirmative and convincing than the conditional (would, could). If the helper uses the present or future tenses the client is more likely to follow. Don't give up too soon on this. Continue asking questions like *'And what else is different?'* to elicit more descriptions of the problem-free state from the client.

4. The stance of the helper has a real impact on the successful use of the Miracle Question. In short, if you don't feel comfortable with it or don't believe that your client can respond to it effectively, then don't use it. It is natural to feel uncertain when using a novel form like this, and the only way to develop confidence is to start using it and to practise. Asking the Miracle Question 'both implies and demands faith in the client's capacity (to create meaningful descriptions)' (de Shazer *et al.* 2007, p.39).

Apprehensions about miracles

Some people who are new to the Miracle Question are apprehensive about using it. I have found both from using the Miracle Question with clients and in training others to use it that those who waiver, fail. Helpers must therefore embrace the question with a degree of confidence and faith in their client to be able to respond, and they must also be attentive to the answers the client gives, co-constructing with them the post-problem description. The question must be asked in a way that says you really want to hear the answer and that you have confidence in the client's ability to answer it (de Shazer *et al.* 2007).

At the beginning of this section I said that there are some misunderstandings about the Miracle Question and its use. I hope I have cleared some of these up. While acknowledging that using this question takes skill, I encourage you to start using it because it will improve with practice and so will you. People sometimes ask me about the limitations of the Miracle Question and I reply by saying that, when used with sensitivity and common sense, questions do not have limitations, any shortcomings will be in the way they are used.

Finally, the ticklish matter of belief in miracles. Those of us who train others in SFBT techniques are familiar with the line 'This would never work with my clients because…' or 'I could never use this with my clients because they (have terminal illness, have lost someone they love…, etc).' This is to misunderstand the Miracle Question.

Clients are also human beings and realists. They know this is a linguistic device and not a literal expectation. If I ask someone the Miracle Question and they respond with 'My doctor would tell me there's been a mistake and I'm not going to die after all,' or 'My husband would be alive and back with me,' these are simply natural, wishful, responses. They do not indicate that the client really expects that to happen. I would simply respond with an acknowledgement and move on. So, to 'My husband would be alive', the helper's response might be, 'Of course… and?', or simply, silence, and after an appropriate pause, 'What else?' Remember that apprehension about this question starts with the therapist. We can ask the question with confidence, and see what happens, or if we are doubtful we can transmit our apprehension to the client…and see what happens.[3]

Questions are intended to initiate a response of some sort, whether this is behaviour, thinking, or some other form of action, and they direct attention and energy (Goldberg 1998). The Miracle Question is the best known of these in SFBT, but there are many other types which are more commonplace and more frequently used. For my part, though I use the Miracle Question often I do not routinely use it with all clients. This is not to invalidate it. In some cases it may seem inappropriate, but far more

---

3   Apprehensively is not the same as tentatively. When dealing with issues about which the client might be particularly sensitive or vulnerable, I would be tentative in my use of the Miracle Question. If the client does not take to it, I drop it, and move on.

often it just doesn't occur to me, as I am usually engrossed in conversation with my client and asking the more day-to-day questions, some of which are listed in the next section.

Goal-setting

It is implicit in the therapeutic relationship that the person in the role of client is seeking at least a sense of direction, if not explicit instructions on how to get somewhere. If we are to accomplish anything with them it is first essential to know what they wish to have happen as a result of our intervention. More specifically, assuming that we are successful, what will be different in their lives?

At this point there are three main questions to be asked:

1. What are their goals?

2. How will they know when they are moving towards it?

3. What needs to happen to get things going in the right directions?

Goal-setting in SFBT is the keystone of the approach and, like their architectural counterpart, these goals have to be built with precision. Many of us are familiar with the concept of setting goals, if not in our daily lives, certainly in our professional activities. Most of us too can vividly recall a time when we failed to achieve a target we had set ourselves, even if the consequences were not too severe. Whatever the outcome, it is likely that we failed because either we had aimed far too high or we had not been specific enough in our aims. Our clients do the same, and they get trapped in a loop. Here's how it works. First, they set themselves a goal which they then fail to attain. Perhaps it was too high to achieve, or it was simply too vague. Either way the result is the same: failure to reach the goal. If it was too high it would be out of reach (so aim for small, achievable goals) and if it is vague or abstract ('North', 'feel better' or 'happy', for example), it would be difficult to recognise, and it would appear elusive (Johnson 1946). Believing they have failed, they are then either discouraged and give up, or they set themselves new goals (using the same flawed method), and promptly fail again. And all this is due to the same basic error: vaguely defined goals to all intents and purposes are unachievable, and unachievable goals appear out of reach.

It is as if, in setting out to drive from the south of England to the north, to visit a friend in Manchester, I simply head north. This will be fine for the first few miles, but the nearer I get to my intended destination the more information I need about where I actually want to wind up. If I can keep in mind that it is Manchester I want, rather than, more vaguely, the north, the more likely I am to be able to plan my route and reach my destination (and once in Manchester, if I don't have an address to head for, the problem starts all over again).

Replace 'the north' with 'feel better' or 'be happy' and we can see immediately why so many people fail to reach their goals. Feeling better or happy are fine as aspirations. These are the sort of abstract concepts people frequently use to describe their ideals to themselves. But how do we know when we are 'happy'? So goals must be specific, realistic:

So goals in SFBT must be clear, concrete and specific, and wherever possible small and achievable to start with. Clients should also be encouraged to describe their goals as solutions – see 'positively stated' below – rather than the absence of the problem (de Shazer *et al.* 2007).

- 'What would you like to have happen as a result of us working together?'
- 'How will you know when you have got there?'
- 'What needs to happen to get things going in the right direction for you?'

It is important to elicit from clients what, for them, would constitute a satisfactory outcome(s) from the collaborative exercise of therapy. This can be translated into goals. Goals should be:

Positively stated

In other words, expressed as the presence, rather than the absence of something. So, a client's wish to 'not be depressed anymore' begs the question 'How will you know when that happens?' The idea is to find out how 'not depressed anymore' can be expressed positively. For example, 'getting up and doing X' or 'I'll be back at work'. Goals must be framed as solutions, not just the absence of the problem.

Realistic

Goals often fail because they are set unrealistically high. In such cases they can have the adverse effect of reinforcing the client's sense of failure. Check that the client has the skills, resources and abilities and will be able to take appropriate steps towards reaching their goals.

Achievable

This puts the goal within the control of the client and means that they can take full credit for their success. Goals must also be important and relevant to the client, and small enough to best ensure success.

Specific

How will we know when the client has started to move towards their goal? Is it measurable, tangible, concrete? Goals must be expressed in specific, behavioural terms. 'To be happy' is a laudable aim, it is not an easily measurable outcome. The way past this is to ask 'How will you know when you are happy?' or 'What will you be doing when you are happy?', thus transforming it into something which is tangible.

Measurable

How will the client (and the therapist) know when goals have been reached? What will be the signs that the client is moving in the right direction?

Other solution focused questions

Here are some examples of SFBT questions to get you started or act as prompts. These are not mine, if they 'belong' to anyone they belong to the SFBT community which freely shares such information.

To elicit need and create expectation

'What brings you here today?'

'Why now?'

'What would you like to have happen?'

'How will you know when it has started?'

'What will you be doing differently?'

'What has helped so far?'

'When does it not happen/happen less, etc.?'

'What positive changes have happened already?'

'How will you know this has been useful?'

'Things don't seem to be going well between you and (name), how would you like it to be different?'

'Imagine that things start to improve, what would you have happen?'

'What is the single, smallest thing you could do to make things easier between you.'

'How will you respond differently when they begin to change?'

'How will he/she respond when you do something different?'

'What will (name) notice different about you when she/he is being different?'

'How could you find your way into a different kind of conversation with (name)?'

'What do you not want to change about them?'

'What do you want to stay the same?'

What is already happening?

'What has changed since you made the appointment/heard you were coming here?'

'What are you already doing that helps?'

'What do you do that makes it easier to talk? Are there times when you do/don't do that?'

'Can you think of times when that is already happening?'

'Have you got a recent example of something you have been successful with?' (plus 'What else, what else, what else?')

Identifying strengths and resources

'What are you good at?'

'What do you like/enjoy doing?'

'If I asked X, what would he/she say?'

'How have you managed to do that?'

'How can you make that happen again?'

'Which of these skills do you use in other parts of your life?'

'When that change is happening, what are you doing?'

'How do you keep going?'

'What helps?' (plus 'What else, what else, what else?')

As well as generally eliciting information, among other things, questions can be used to:

Clarify a situation

'Tell me more about that, what do you mean?'

'You said that she "acted differently" towards you. What exactly happened?'

Create a sense of expectation

'What would you like to have happen?'

'How will things be different for you as they start to improve?'

Instil the idea of a fresh start (in therapy):

'Given that you have seen so many different people for help with this, what makes this situation different?'

'You've already done a lot of work on this, what shall we focus on?'

Inform the client that the process is time limited

'So how will things be different when we have finished working together?'

'How much time (how many sessions) do you think we could reasonably spend on this?'

Issuing a challenge:

'You say that your teenage son is not normal, how would you say that a normal teenager acts?'

'As a total failure you must have worked hard to get your degree. How did you manage that?'

Direct the client's attention to exceptions to the problem

'At what times do you manage to get along with him without arguing?'

'What are you doing when the panic attacks don't occur?'

Suggest that the client has hidden resources

'Given that this is so difficult for you, how have you managed so well so far?'

'On the days you manage to go to work, what's the trick you use to keep the depression from getting to you?'

Offer a different perspective (reframe the client's behaviour)

'You've been pretty hard on yourself, what would your spouse/friend/boss/children say about you?'

'Given that you say you are a workaholic, how do you manage to spend so much time with your daughter?'

Refocus the client's attention on the positive

'What will be the first little signs that things might be moving in the right direction?'

'What positive changes have you noticed?'

Empower the client

'After the nightmarish experiences you have faced together, what have you learned about your relationship?'

'How did you manage to come through it despite all the predictions they made about you?'

Link events (that the client may have seen as 'chance') to their efforts

'How did you get that to happen?'

'How do you do that?'

Move from the vague to the specific

'You said you get "depressed". What actually happens when you are depressed?'

'You said that "everyone knows", could you explain it to me, so I understand?'

Establish an initial point of focus

'If we could only do one thing today, what would it be?'

'Which bits will sort themselves out if we let them?'

Identify existing skills

'You mentioned that you had a similar difficulty in the past, how did you resolve it then?'

'If you were advising someone else with this problem, what would you suggest they do?'

Uncover limiting or inconsistent values and beliefs

'You said that it "runs in the family". What do you mean by that exactly?'

'I agree that loyalty is important in a person. Would you say that it is a one-way or a two-way process?'

Responding to objections

Client:	That will never happen.
Therapist:	That bad eh? If we could change one bit of it today, what would it be? *OR:* OK, so what are your hopes for this call?
Client:	I'm giving up, I'll drop out next term.
Therapist:	I guess that's a possibility; anything we could do to help in the meantime?
Client:	I've tried everything.
Therapist:	Sounds like a tough one, how can I help?
Client:	What's the point, they'll never change.
Therapist:	I see, if one thing could change, what would it be?

Answer emphatic statements with an acknowledgement, and then a question.

These are just a few examples and, as you will probably have spotted, many actually do several things at once. For example, as well as informing the client that the process of therapy is time limited, 'How will things be different when we have finished working together?' also presupposes that change can happen (*things will be different*), and that the relationship is collaborative (*we...working together*). In asking such questions we are also encouraging the client to think differently about their experience and develop new thinking habits.

Questions are a powerful and generally under-used device. Deployed with skill and imagination they can be considered as interventions in their own right. Of course, therapy sessions generally consist of a wide varied number of interactions, not just questions. But a usefully placed question can be worth more than hours of directionless discussion.

Clients regularly testify to this. I once asked a man who I'll call Bob, ten minutes into his fifth session, 'What do we need to do today?' He replied 'We just did it with a question you asked a few minutes ago.' After a brief discussion and a few jokes we agreed to end the session at that point since he said that was all he needed 'for now'.

Bob had been struggling with his drink problem for twenty years. He had been in and out of treatment for a long time, including several spells at expensive clinics, without much success. During our first few sessions together he was pleased that he had his habit under control and had stopped drinking secretly while the family slept. He had also noticed a number of positive changes in his relationships. But he was unconvinced that the changes would last. I asked him, 'You've consulted the best in the last 20 years, you kept going back despite, as you say, your lousy success rate. Where do you get your optimism and tenacity from?'

While I intended the question to set him thinking and reframe his perceived 'lousy success rate' as tenacity and persistence, I had not expected the question to have any special significance for him. His answer, 'I don't know,' seemed to confirm this and I hadn't pursued it at the time. In our brief discussion that concluded the session that day Bob told me that this question would give him 'food for thought', and that he'd like to reflect on it for a while.

We may never know the value of the questions we ask, but we should never underestimate the profound effect they can have. They frequently live on in the client's mind long after the moment when they were asked. Use them to practise and develop your own questioning skills, and remember, one well-placed question can be worth hours of aimless therapy-talk.

Solution focused questions will take the conversation towards solutions, whereas problem focused questions will take the conversation in the opposite direction. While they both have their place, choosing how and when to use each is critical.

CHAPTER 9

The First SFBT Session

Helpers meet and work with their clients in a wide variety of settings and many of these do not fit with the typical therapy format of 50- or 60-minute sessions on a regular basis. SFBT is widely used in education, social welfare, prisons, healthcare and other situations where practitioners use counselling skills in the normal course of their work, but would never consider themselves as counsellors and may not even have the opportunity of regular meetings with their service users. Client groups include:

- psychiatric patients
- prison inmates
- drug users
- carers and families
- refugees and asylum seekers
- children with educational difficulties
- adults and children in healthcare
- children and adults in child protection
- people with eating disorders
- employee support programmes
- homeless people.

Because of its conversational nature – Furman and Ahola call it 'a constructive and agreeable manner of talking to people about problems' (1992, p.xxiv) – SFBT lends itself to working in a loose and unstructured way that can be fitted into any working routine. In order to describe a first session I shall be suggesting a structure, and this is also inevitable for teaching and learning purposes. Most of us, when we learn something new, would rather have a framework to guide us but, equally, most of us, once we have mastered something, will begin to adapt it to our own way of working. The following is therefore a suggested session structure, how you will use it will depend on the requirements and possibilities of your working context.

As we have seen, the quality of the working relationship is a basic requirement and I would always prefer to establish what I refer to as a robust working relationship at the outset. Though I take this as a given in any helping relationship, productive work cannot really begin until some sort of therapeutic alliance has been established (Battino 2006; Frank and Frank 1991), I also know this is not always possible. In some settings – child protection and probation, for example – practitioners are required to work with people who do not welcome their attention. In such cases it takes time to build trust and the necessary rapport in order to work collaboratively, but this does not mean that the basic SFBT ideas cannot be used. On the contrary, it just means treading more carefully while the relationship is developing. If you are working with 'involuntary clients', those who have been ordered to see you by a court or other agency, there is literature on how you might approach this, see, for example, Miller, Hubble and Duncan 1996; Turnell and Edwards 1999; Walter and Peller 1992.

Session structure

I have broken the session into several 'steps'. Many of these overlap and taking a common-sense approach the order in which they are used is not critical. In practice some of them are not steps at all. Identifying strengths, looking for resources, asking about exceptions and creating goals are all features of SF conversations and happen throughout the session.

- Introduction
- Problem-free talk
- Defining the problem
- The Miracle Question
- Goal-setting
- Identify strengths and resources
- Exceptions to the problem
- Pre-session change
- The message
- Homework

Introduction

Starting a session with a client that one has not met before obviously requires the normal introductions and a bit of rapport-building chit-chat. Since nothing is wasted in SFBT, even apparently banal chit-chat is useful to SF practitioners. As well as helping to break the ice and put the client at their ease, it also provides information about the client – how they dress and conduct themselves, how they got to the session, were they on time? – that demonstrates abilities and resources which may later feature in the session.

Right from the start of the session, while listening empathetically and acknowledging the client's story, we are also listening for possibilities: possibilities of other versions of the story; of things the client has missed; and for nuggets of information and evidence of skills that can be fashioned into resources on which to build solutions. I have already referred to this as 'listening with the third ear' (Chapter 8). For example, with a client who is speaking about being handicapped by marital disputes, we can listen out for times when their relationship functioned more harmoniously, or when they managed to achieve something together despite the tensions. If they do this sometimes and we can find out the context or what enabled them to act in this way, this enables us to build an alternative picture, and information we can later reintroduce into the conversation. 'As therapists, we need to develop eyes and ears that are flexible in perceiving, and sensitive to non-problem times and behaviours, so that we and the clients can more easily elicit the non-problem times' (Walter and Peller 1992, p.17). Nothing is wasted, even though at this stage of the session the work of 'therapy' may not have yet started. SF practitioners are constantly on the lookout for evidence of exceptions to the problem.

This general discussion leads into what is known in SF terminology as 'problem-free talk' (Henden 2008; O'Connell and Palmer 2003).

Problem-free talk

Problem-free talk involves conversation on topics unrelated to the problem. This might be about the client's passions and pursuits, travel or holidays, family…whatever presents itself. This is not like idle small-talk one might engage in at a party; the helper shows intelligent interest in what is being said and curiosity about the person they have just met. It may seem strange to the client, who has come along to discuss their problems, only to find one of the first questions is about how they spend their free time, but people respond to it well and it helps set the scene and establish a degree of equality. After all this is to be a collaborative relationship. It also says to the client, in effect, that there is more to them than the problem that brought them along. It is a rapport builder and gives the helper an opportunity to listen out for strengths, skills and resources before launching into 'the problem' (Henden 2008).

The drift into problem-free talk is, in my experience, usually seamless and circumstances often dictate the topic (as I write this we are gearing up for the World Cup, summer holidays are almost upon us, hot weather is forecast for the weekend). If it doesn't happen naturally then we can always prime the conversations with a question or two, such as:

'How do you like to spend your spare time?'

'Have you lived long in this area?'

'Where do you like to go for your holidays?'

Defining the problem

As Jay Haley says, 'therapy starts by negotiating a solvable problem' (Haley 1976, p.3). Until we know what it is the client wants to change we cannot be much use to them, nor they to themselves. And Haley's words are chosen carefully when he speaks about 'negotiating a solvable problem', for not all problems are solvable. It is critical how we define, in collaboration with the client, what it is they want to work on and their goals.

If the client says 'I'm depressed and my partner and I are arguing all the time,' the questions we ask in response will decide how accurately and how quickly we help the client define both the problem they want to tackle and their goal(s) for the time we spend together. My question at this point is some variation of 'What brings you here?' (the problem). This then leads on to what the client hopes for as a result of us working together (the solution).

In the above example the problem may be depression, arguments with their partner or something else entirely unrelated. We cannot assume and we won't know until we ask. Attention to detail at this point is important if we are to avoid aimlessness later in the session. Where the client lists multiple problems or is unclear about just what the problem is, then a useful question would be 'If we could only work on one thing today what would it be?', or, 'What shall we start with?'

SFBT is not problem-phobic. There is no rule forbidding the client to describe and explore their difficulties fully. We simply don't dwell on it. Once the client has described the problem, encouraged by the helper's diligent and intelligent questions, they are normally ready to move on to solution-talk and engaging in the process of change. In the few cases where clients need to keep returning to 'problem-talk' I recommend two things:

1. Why do any of us repeat ourselves? Because we feel we have not been heard. If the client is repeatedly going over old ground this may be why. Check this out with 'I notice we keep returning to this question of (X). I am wondering if I have missed something?' I would then add a brief summary of my understanding of the situation they have described. Ask questions to clarify, acknowledge and validate the client's difficulties and concerns where possible.

2. If the repetitions persist you may need to establish a time-limit on problem-talk. I would say something like 'I notice that we spend quite a bit of time on this question of (X). I'm happy to talk about it but I also need to do my job (which, in my case, the client is paying me to do). Can I suggest that we continue to talk about this up to the half-way mark (in the session), and then I can do my bit?'

My job is to use the SF framework to enable the client to design and implement the change they seek. To do this I need to lead them away from problem-talk and towards more fruitful solution-talk (de Shazer 1994; Furman and Ahola 1992). John Henden has refined this to what he calls 'the 5 o'clock rule', which allows the client about 25 minutes of the hour to describe their problems. Henden (2008) says it is helpful at this point to ask clarifying questions to 'acknowledge and validate (the client's) concerns as much as possible', and to demonstrate that the therapist is hearing the client out and trying their best to understand.

Any attempts to move the client towards 'solution-talk' in this way must always be handled with due sensitivity, allowing the time necessary for them to complete their story. One final strategy I have used with people who still persist in returning to the problem is to allow them some defined space to do this on the understanding that we can then return to more productive solution focused discussions at subsequent sessions. I will allocate a session (open ended in time if necessary) to talk only about the problem, during which I will be entirely problem focused, summarising regularly and concluding with a statement which (I hope), demonstrates that I have heard everything, and checking whether they need to say any more before 'laying the problem to rest'. This is symbolic as well as practical and can help free the client from the need to constantly return to the problem during sessions. Alternatively I will set a homework assignment of writing the problem out in detail and bringing the result to the next session. I then ask them what needs to happen to their written account. Do I need to read it, or shall we create a ritual for disposing of it?

When discussing what the client wants to achieve, though the SF approach talks about 'goals', I tend to discuss 'preferred outcomes' or simply ask the client what they would like to have happen as a result of us working together. Incidentally, in line with the SF ethos, all the questions below presuppose success as well as drawing out information:

'What brings you here?'

'What would you like to have happen as a result of (today; these sessions)?'

'How will you know when you won't need to see me any more?' (This presupposes both progress and an end point to therapy, which in turn suggests an outcome.)

The Miracle Question

When the helper has gathered an idea of the problem, and initial rapport with the client has been more or less established, it can be useful to ask the Miracle Question. I have already described this in some detail (Chapter 8). Despite its apparent simplicity this question usually opens up a wealth of possibilities and brings out new information.

Helpers who are new to this sometimes find the Miracle Question daunting, but gentle yet persistent questioning pays off as the client gradually starts to paint a more detailed picture as they imagine waking one post-problem morning:

> This might seem like a strange question, but let's see where it takes us. Imagine that tonight, while you are asleep, a miracle happens. When you wake up, the problem that brought you here has gone. Because you were asleep, you will not know that the miracle has happened, but somehow you know that the problem has gone. How will you know? What will tell you it has gone? What will be different?

Goal-setting

I have covered goal-setting in some detail in previous chapters. Goals probably start to coalesce quite naturally in the conversation, but they usually need some refining, guided by the therapist or helper, to make them satisfactory and achievable. The more carefully the goals are defined the more likely it is that the client will reach them. By carefully, I mean that it is implicit in the role of helper or therapist to ensure that the client doesn't aim too high. Aspirations are fine, whereas unachievable goals simply set them up for failure. One of the cardinal rules in goal-setting is to start small (O'Hanlon and Weiner-Davis 1989), hence questions like 'What would be the first sign that you are moving towards the changes you want?' I quite often suggest that clients 'downgrade' their initial goals. Better one step at a time than to stumble and fall because the goal was too ambitious (see the Appendix for an example of this).

Goal-refining questions are:

'What will make these sessions worthwhile for you?'

'What will you be doing differently when we have finished working together?'

'What would need to change in the next week or so for you to feel we are moving in the right direction?'

'How will you know?'

Another reason that goals fail is that people often couch them in negative terms; they say what they don't want rather than what they do.

Negative: I want to stop smoking.
Solution focused: You'd like to become a non-smoker.

Negative: My husband and I won't be arguing the whole time.
Solution focused: Your relationship will be more peaceful.

Negative: I won't be cooped up in the house all day.
Solution focused: You'll be getting out more.

The standard solution focused response to negative statements like this is to ask another question:

Negative: My husband and I won't be arguing the whole time.
Solution focused: And what *will* you be doing when you are not arguing the whole time?

Negative: I won't be cooped up in the house all day.
Solution focused: So what does 'not cooped up' mean, what will you be
                    doing instead?

Progress towards goals should be reviewed session by session and adjustments made as necessary. Situations change and as they feel they are making even small progress in their lives, clients may decide to re-set their goals. Subject to them still being well defined as above this is fine; they are the client's goals, after all.

The last word on Solution Focused goals goes to de Shazer *et al.*:

> ...clear, concrete and specific goals are an important component of SFBT. Whenever possible, the therapist tries to elicit smaller goals rather than larger ones. More important, clients are encouraged to frame their goals as a solution, rather than the absence of a problem. (2007, p.6)

Identify strengths and resources

SF practitioners constantly have their radar tuned to look for strengths and resources that the client may have missed. SFBT sees clients as resourceful and functioning so, however hopelessly they themselves might view their situation, when we listen carefully they also provide evidence which balances this with examples of successes and exceptions – they just forget to notice it!

These may be particular skills or abilities they possess, people they know, experiences they have had or obstacles they have surmounted. Looking out for these starts as soon as the client makes their first contact, whether it is face-to-face or by telephone. Part of the job-description for SF practitioners is an unstinting curiosity about how people manage adversity and the skills and strengths they bring to it. This curiosity is invaluable for deepening the therapist's understanding of the client's situation and the development of solutions (de Shazer *et al.* 2007). The stance of sincere and attentive listening, combined with the occasional summary, and even a reframe or two lets the client not only know that they have been heard and understood, but also lets them know that some 'old complaint' is in fact evidence of strengths they didn't know they had or had forgotten.

Exceptions to the problem

Although these are described as discrete steps here, in practice the SF helper weaves several things together into a conversation about change that Bill O'Connell called the 'change discourse' (1998, p.35). Identifying strengths, affirming skills, enquiring about exceptions, understanding resources and constructing solutions are all part of 'solution-talk'.

Exceptions to the problem are those times when the problem doesn't occur, when it happens but is not so troublesome, or when it did occur and was managed better. Clients who are locked into a problem mindset fail to see balancing aspects such as these, or, if they do notice, will dismiss them in some way. The aim is to identify the unnoticed or undervalued incidents in the search for hidden resources. Identifying exceptions does a number of things:

- It punctuates the monotony of 'problem-talk' with some counter-examples.

- It demonstrates critical thinking to the client, thus modelling a style of thinking they might benefit from.

- It provides evidence of exceptions where a problem has seemed all pervasive.

- It can be used as evidence of client resourcefulness.

- Previous successes can be noticed and similar strategies perhaps used again.

- It reframes the client's story, or parts of it, as far more multifaceted than they had probably considered.

- It starts to chip away the monolith of self-doubt, failure or negative belief surrounding 'the problem'.

- It can affirm the client and lift their spirits.

Client: We argue all the time.

Therapist: And what do you do in between the arguments?

Client: We don't speak.

Therapist: So, how much of the time do you spend not speaking?

Client: About half the evening.

Therapist: In an average evening of, say, six hours, you manage not to argue for up to three of them?

Client: I suppose that's true.

Therapist: How do you manage that? I mean, it's really hard to walk away from an argument.

In this brief exchange we have rendered the situation less desperate, potentially more manageable and have possibly identified skills like walking away from an argument, self-soothing and the ability to call a truce. Who knows what further clarification would reveal?

Some newcomers to SFBT worry that focusing on exceptions might seem disrespectful to clients. After all, interrupting them in mid-flow with their problems to ask strange questions about problem-free times might seem uncaring and insensitive. This is a natural anxiety but it says more about practitioner apprehension than it does about client receptivity. Helpers and therapists used to the SF approach do not experience any resistance to these questions. If you are concerned about this bear in mind that the search for exceptions is in the context of a robust helper/client relationship which will support the therapist's bizarre ways. It is also worth remembering that clients come to us for help, which means that we are probably going to do something different. They can always stick with their problem-talk on their own time. When people come for help (and in some cases pay for it) they usually expect to do something different.

Pre-session change

From an SF perspective change is happening all the time, small change can lead to bigger (positive) change and problems can be viewed as an inevitable side-effect of living. Since nothing is constant, it doesn't make sense that positive change only starts to happen when the client walks into a therapist's office. Perhaps it has already started? We had better ask.

It is known from studies in family therapy, general practice and elsewhere that, when asked about positive change that may have happened *prior* to the session, between 15 and 66 per cent of clients report some positive improvement in relation to the problem that they are seeking help with (Bertolino 2003; McKeel 1996; O'Hanlon and Weiner-Davis 1989). Furthermore, studies say, clients who report pre-session change are more likely to finish treatment with a successful outcome. The crucial word here is 'report', because 'Additionally, pretreatment change is a phenomenon that is constructed in the conversation that occurs during the session. As such, pretreatment change only begins to be relevant to the client after talking about it with the therapist' (Beyebach *et al.* 1996, pp.322–3).

At some point early in the session it is worth asking the client if they have noticed any such changes between the time the appointment was made and the time they attend the first session. If, for any reason, it is not appropriate to ask this (for example, if things have been so diabolically difficult for the client that such a question would sound insensitive), then the helper should listen and ask about things that the client has done for themselves during the interim. The rationale here is that knowing they are going to see a therapist or helper can motivate clients to start to plan or make changes for themselves.

In either case – small spontaneous changes the client may notice or things they have done for themselves – I would acknowledge this and ask them how they managed to bring about the change. ('How did you manage to do that?') Even if the change was spontaneous it is useful to link it, in the client's mind, to the idea that they may in some way have influenced events, even if they didn't directly carry them out. Acknowledgement in this way associates change to action and thereby increases the client's sense of personal agency. It also sets the scene for what is to follow (O'Connell and Palmer 2003).

Given the opportunity some SF practitioners will set up expectation when the client books the appointment by saying something like 'Between now and our first session, I want you to notice the things that happen to you that you would like to keep happening to you in the future. In this way you will help me to find out more about your goal and what you are up to' (Talmon 1990, p.19). According to Talmon this contains several messages:

that the therapist is interested in naturally occurring and effortless changes ('Notice what happens to you')

that the focus is on the transition from the present to the future ('Between now and out first session')

that the client is active and collaborating in their treatment ('You will help me'). (p.19)

In addition this type of question also encourages clients to break their habitual problem focused way of thinking, challenging some of their negative 'certainties' and generally loosening things up in anticipation of their new working relationship with the helper. Incidentally, it doesn't harm the helper's relationship that they are able to anticipate change happening before therapy even starts!

What could go wrong?

It may seem odd to ask this in a session devoted to co-constructing solutions. Ask it we must, though, and here's why. As the session progresses clients typically become more comfortable with solution-talk. By the end of the session, when asked, clients often say they are feeling a little more optimistic, and so clearly we would like them to end on a high note (at least a little higher than where they were at the start of the session). Before leaving them with a message which we hope will inspire and motivate them though, there is one last thing we must check and we do it by asking some version of the question above:

Therapist: What could go wrong?

Client: I suppose I might oversleep one morning and get into trouble at work again. That would really bring me down.

Therapist: So what precautions might you take, to make sure you can get up in time?

Client: I sometimes forget to set the alarm, if I make a point of doing that it'll help. I could book myself an alarm call as backup too.

Therapist: And that would work for you.

Client: It has in the past, so yes.

(Equally, in this scenario, the helper might discuss how the client would manage if they did oversleep. Keep it brief though to avoid the conversation turning back into problem-talk.)

Or:

Therapist: We've had an instructive session (for helper and client) and you have developed some useful ideas about how you will (start to reduce your drinking). I was just wondering though, before we wind up, whether anything could go wrong? I know you said that you feel pretty upbeat now, and that you can (begin to make the changes that we discussed during the session), but you know how it is, sometimes our best intentions are stymied by unexpected events. I'm wondering if anything could happen to get in the way of your new plan?

Client: What could go wrong? What usually starts me off is that I get fed up because I have had a bad day at work. So I guess if I had a really bad day, I might want to get myself a drink. If I'm in a bad mood I don't stop at one drink, so that might start me off again.

Therapist: Let's hope it doesn't happen, but what if you do have a bad day? What could you do differently so you can keep the drinking at bay?

Client: Like I said earlier, I tend not to drink as much when I've been to the gym, so if I come out of work feeling lousy I could go straight to the gym.

Therapist: And how would you know, that you feel lousy I mean?

Client: I could ask myself how I'm feeling when I leave work, say on a scale of 1 to 10 like you showed me. I know that below 5 is a problem, so if I'm below 5 that could be my signal to go to the gym.

Therapist: As you mentioned scaling, how confident are you, on a scale of 1 to 10, that that you could do that?

Client: Right now? Seven or eight, pretty confident, I just need to think about it when I leave work.

The rationale here is to get the client to do a 'reality-check'. This reduces the likelihood that 'real life' outside the session will seriously disrupt the client's progress. For there is a real probability that this will happen. David Liddle, a London-based colleague who works in conflict resolution, when asked during lectures how many of his cases fail, likes to say '100%! We get a resolution in almost all our cases, but conflict doesn't go away and people in dispute are bound to argue again. The difference is in how they deal with it. After our intervention they can handle it constructively' (personal communication).

This is echoed in other fields, marital therapy and mediation, for example. Psychologist and marital therapist John Gottman says of couples in dispute that 69 per cent of the time they were talking about a 'perpetual problem' that they had had in their marriage for many, many years, and that 'Only 31% of the discussions involved situationally specific problem-solving' (1999, p.56).

In other words, some problems don't go away just because clients enter therapy. What happens in many cases where therapy is successful is that clients learn to handle their problems more effectively.

As clients work towards their goals, building on the solutions that have emerged or been constructed during therapy, to assume that progress will be smooth would not only be unrealistic, it would be foolhardy and irresponsible on the part of the therapist. 'What could go wrong?' asks clients to look into the future so that we can help them prepare for the inevitable hiccups. It also frames the odd setback as a normal part of progress which helper and client, together, have anticipated.

The message

An SFBT session usually ends with a summary and prescription. The summary consists of things the helper has heard that suggest competence, success, positive intentions and ways in which the client has met any challenges (Berg and Dolan 2001). Originally this idea came from family therapy where the therapist would step outside the room to confer with his or her colleagues, who would have been watching the session from behind a one-way mirror (O'Hanlon and Weiner-Davis 1989). Some SFBT practitioners still take themselves out of the room for a few minutes, but most simply take a short break in the session to think about what has been said and to reflect on feedback they will give to the client (O'Connell and Palmer 2003).

This break enables the helper to prepare the 'message' for the client in which the helper recounts their version of the session, highlighting example of strengths, skills and other resources that have come to light during the conversation, in effect reframing the client's story and complimenting them on those things which the client is already doing that are working for them. It also serves as a 'context marker' (O'Hanlon and Weiner-Davis 1989), which indicates a new phase in the session, increases expectation and in effect says to the client 'please sit up and take note'. In my sessions I often notice that at this point clients actually begin to demonstrate greater attentiveness non-verbally, by sitting up straighter and leaning forward slightly.

The helper then presents the message, which concludes the session and consists of:

- thanking the client for coming to the session and acknowledging their participation and willingness to share; complimenting them on some aspect of their attitude or behaviour

- a short summary including what the helper feels about the session and the client's resourcefulness, including reframing and normalisation of the client's responses to their problem

- amplification of any information the helper has gleaned that demonstrates resourcefulness on the part of the client

- confirmation of goals and the steps needed to move towards them as agreed during the session

- a 'homework' task or assignment.

The purpose of the message is to end the session on a high note with specific instructions – a prescription – on something the client can do to continue the work (see *Homework*, below). The message enables the client to take a number of things away from the session with them:

- a new interpretation of their situation, in which they are seen as someone who is resourceful, doing their best and, though they hadn't noticed it before the session, making progress through their own agency

- the notion that some of the things they have been doing have been working, as evidenced by pre-session change and other information gleaned during the session

- a sense of anticipation that positive change will continue to happen

- a course of action derived from the conversation during the session, built on doing more of what is working for them, other specific steps agreed during the session and a homework assignment

- an explanation or rationale for the course of action, though in practice I find that many clients do not need this or infer their own rationale from what they are agreeing to do.

Walter and Peller say that this feedback is organised around four purposes. These are educational, consisting of information that will help the client think differently about their courses of action or solution; normalising, including compliments about how they have been managing so far, and de-pathologising their situation or any labels (for example anger problems, family dysfunction, etc.), that they brought to the session with them; alternative meaning, drawn from reframes or the therapist's 'expert' understanding of situations like theirs; and a rationale, or basis for chosen courses of action, based on the SFBT rule 'if it works, do more of it' (1992, pp.123–4).

Example of closing statement (message)

'First I'd like to thank you for coming today, and for sharing with me the things you have told me about. It's not easy coming somewhere new like this and discussing these things, and I must compliment you on coming in here and getting on with it. I'm impressed with your insights about what you might do to get a greater degree of control over the problem. You have helped me understand your situation and how you have been tackling it and I hope maybe I've given you a few ideas as well.

A couple of things I've noticed are that you seem very keen to find ways of leaving your depression behind, and the fact that you've already been able to do this on a number of occasions makes me confident that you'll be able to continue and do more of the things that are helpful. For example, you said that you are never aware of the rumination when you are walking to and from work, and that you seem to feel a little better on those days as well. You also said that you sleep better if you start to wind down with a book an hour or so before bed, rather than catching up on chores or playing computer games. We talked about you walking to work at least three days a week, and making a habit of reading before bed, so fixing a cut-off time of around 8.30–9.00 for the other things.

You said that you have been as low as -4 on your scale of comfort with yourself, and that today you are on a +5. That's a tremendous indicator of progress. No-hopers just don't make progress like that, and you are to be congratulated on working at it. I know you attributed some of that to the fact that you had decided to talk to someone about this (the helper), and to me that just reaffirms what I said earlier about your ability to move towards your goals of feeling confident enough to start looking for a new job.

We have agreed to see each other in a couple of weeks, and I'll look forward to hearing about how things are going for you then. In the meantime, I'd just ask you to look out for any positive changes that begin to show themselves, and let me know about anything you notice when we meet.'

This sort of statement allows the helper to amplify any positive messages from the session and to reinforce any changes in the client's perceptions. As it is set apart from the rest of the session, it is seen as important and conclusive (O'Hanlon and Weiner-Davis 1989). Homework tasks flow naturally from this and are aimed at furthering construction of the solutions (Walter and Peller 1992, p.124).

Homework

Homework assignments or tasking are used to carry the work forward and to act as a bridge between sessions. These fall broadly into two categories. The Formula First Session Task (FFST), formulated by Steve de Shazer, follows, as the name suggests, a standard wording irrespective of the goals the client has formulated. The FFST is deliberately vague, orienting the client towards noticing positive change. De Shazer called this a 'skeleton key intervention': 'Between now and the next time we meet, I would like you to observe, so you can describe to me the next time, what happens in your (family, life, marriage, relationship) that you want to continue to have happen' (1985, p.137).

As with the Miracle Question, I recommend that practitioners new to the FFST stick to the standard wording until they are familiar and comfortable with using it. After that it may be shortened or adapted slightly. For example I routinely ask clients to 'look out for any positive changes that occur' before the next session.

The second category consists of personalised, goal-related tasks that generally suggest themselves during the session and arise out of discussions about solutions, as in the example above. 'In the meantime, I'd just ask you to look out for any positive changes that begin to show themselves, and let me know about anything you notice when we meet.' These tasks frequently revolve around 'noticing' and/or 'doing more of the same'. They are aimed at furthering the construction of solutions (Walter and Peller 1992). Basic SFBT tasks instruct clients to:

- Look out for the positives: 'Between now and the next session, look out for any small, positive changes.'

- Notice how and when exceptions are happening: 'As you go through the (week), notice any times when the problem doesn't happen, or when it happens but doesn't bother you.'

- Do more of the exceptions or re-create problem-free times: 'Look out for opportunities to do the things you mentioned (during the session) that mean you are problem-free or that the problem is less intrusive.'

- Practise some new behaviour that would be part of the solution: 'You mentioned that one of your goals is to get out more, maybe go to the cinema. I'm wondering if you could mentally rehearse that, say, by looking at the listings and planning a trip to the movies, even though you are not ready to go yet.' Or, 'I'm struck by what you said about wishing you could walk away from an argument at home, yet you are seen as a peacekeeper at work. Perhaps you could spend some time reflecting on how you might introduce some of that work skill at home.'

Generalised tasks like the FFST may be used with anyone who takes to them, but if the client fails to understand or is not keen to accept the homework task then don't insist. Goal-related tasks should be designed to fit the client. Ideas for these generally emerge naturally during the session. These use something the client wants to achieve, something they are doing already that is helping, or something new they want to learn and are prepared to have a shot at. In the latter case it is extremely important to start small, making sure that the task is within the client's range of abilities. For example, with a couple who argue constantly, rather than setting a task of 'calling a halt to the argument' (not many of us can manage that), it is fairer and they are more likely to be able to comply if we suggest 'notice the times when you start to argue but it doesn't develop into a blazing row, and think about how that happens.' Like goals, small and achievable tasks are safer and more respectful to the client than ambitious tasks which they either won't do or will fail at. Incidentally, at follow-up sessions the helper should always congratulate the client on their tasks and findings, so they get the credit for success. In the event that the client has not completed the task or has, as they see it 'failed', it is a good idea for the helper to take responsibility for this by saying that they had not prepared the task carefully enough, or something similar, because it would be counter-therapeutic for the client to attribute failure to themselves.

Finally, and perhaps oddest of all, clients do not have to carry out their tasks. Most will, and even if when asked at the next session they say there has been no change, further discussion invariably demonstrates movement. If, however, the client has not carried out their task, no problem. Accept this as information and move on. I never use the word homework – though that is in the SFBT terminology – preferring 'task', 'assignment' or 'project' – because of the classroom connotations and the implications of not doing one's homework (punishment, detention, etc). Doing tasks is optional and voluntary, there should be no pressure or insistence.

Conclusion

In this section I have provided a step-by-step guide to a solution focused intervention though, as I have explained, the 'steps' are by way of explanation, and this does not mean that each step has to be slavishly followed. Describing a 'session' in a structured way is necessary, but this is not to suggest that the steps must be adhered to rigidly in this order, or even at all. In practice they are not used in any particular order, but as need and opportunity arise, drawing on all the linguistic devices I have described to help the client transform the meaning of their experience and in some cases their lives.

Solution Focused Brief Therapy has been called a 'living process' developed by listening to feedback from clients (Bliss and Bray 2009). This sets it apart from most other forms of therapeutic exercise by engaging the client collaboratively, as an expert in their own lives, and co-creator of solutions and their goals.

SF therapists and helpers are required to take what their clients say seriously, and to learn and use their language and frames of reference. They must notice and name the skills and abilities manifest in the client's descriptions, seek aspects of their stories which give clues to strengths and compliment them on the positive qualities that these indicate (Bliss and Bray 2009).

SFBT sessions are engaging, collaborative, active, future focused and enlivened affairs in which both helper and client work harder than they might appear to on the surface. For all of this, we must keep in mind the essential simplicity of SFBT. Our job as practitioners is to master the techniques and to practise them lightly; keeping things simple without attempting to theorise or provide explanations about problems or their solutions.

Exercise

This is an exercise described by Steve de Shazer, in *Words Were Originally Magic* (1994, pp.66–67). He asks us to envisage an experiment: 'Imagine that you have spent the last half hour talking to Mr A about all the problems in his life, focusing particularly on his feelings of depression. How do you feel after that half hour?'

For the second part of the experiment de Shazer asks us to: 'Imagine that you have spent the last half hour talking to Mr B about all the things that have gone well in his life, focusing particularly on his feelings of success. How do you feel after that half hour?'

I use a version of this in my workshops that enables participants to quickly 'get' the difference between these two modes of discussion:

1. Work with a colleague or friend for this exercise and allow about 20 minutes for each of you to experience both 'roles', designated person 'A' and person 'B'. Use some sort of timer, a kitchen timer is ideal, which you can set without the distraction of having to 'timekeep'.

2. Person A thinks of a difficulty or irritant in their life that they have been unable to change. This might be their own or someone else's behaviour, a habit or intrusive thinking pattern (avoid major trauma or events where you are still highly emotionally aroused, like an argument you had this morning, for example).

3. Person B takes the role of questioner. Set the timer for 10 minutes. Person B is only allowed to ask problem focused questions, such as 'What's the problem?', 'How long have you had it?', 'How does it inconvenience you?', 'How do you feel about it?', etc. Person B can *only* ask questions to clarify his/her understanding of the problem. No suggestions, discussion or helpful comments. Only problem focused questions are allowed. Keep this up for 10 minutes.

4. When the timer rings, stop immediately. No further discussion. Both participants to silently note how they feel, and to scale their level of optimism: 'How hopeful are you, on a scale of 1 to 10, that Person A can make significant change to the problem they have discussed over the next two weeks?'

5. Note where you are on the scale and keep it to yourself. Do not discuss it yet.

6. Now switch to solution-talk. Person B asks SF questions like: 'When does the problem not happen?', 'Tell me about the times when you

forget about it?', 'Are there any times when it happens but it doesn't bother/inconvenience you?', 'If one positive thing could happen in relation to this problem, what would it be?'

Ask the Miracle Question, 'What would tell you the problem has gone?', 'What else?', 'What else…?'

Person B can ask *only* SF questions to uncover exceptions, problem-free times, resources, skills and other assets that Person A has not noticed or has disregarded. Once again, no suggestions, discussion or helpful comments. Only solution focused questions are allowed. Keep this up for 10 minutes.

7. Ask the same question again: 'How hopeful are you, on a scale of 1 to 10, that Person A can make significant change to the problem they have discussed over the next two weeks?'

8. Note where you are on the scale. Is there a difference between the problem and solution focused scores? Notice too how you feel after the second questioning exercise compared with the first. Discuss and compare.

When I run this in my workshops, participants tell me that they feel lighter, they discover strengths and resources they never knew the 'client' had and the likelihood of moving forward seems more tangible and real.

CHAPTER 10

The Helping Relationship

The raison d'être of the helping professionals is to build and maintain a supportive relationship and, from there, to help those they care for maintain or improve their quality of life. Egan (1994) says that the goals in helping are:

- to help clients manage their problems in living more effectively and develop unused or underused opportunities more fully

- to help clients become better at helping themselves in their everyday lives.

These aims chime well with SFBT perspectives, for example, to 'identify and amplify change' (O'Hanlon and Weiner-Davis 1989), or to 'build upon client's resources…to help clients achieve their preferred outcomes by evoking and co-constructing solutions to their problems' (O'Connell and Palmer 2003, p.2), and 'a way of thinking, a way of conversing and a way of interacting with clients' (Walter and Peller 1992, p.35), through 'the pragmatics of hope and respect' (Berg and Dolan 2001).

If our aim as helpers is to enable clients to have a better quality of life through a greater sense of their own agency and abilities, then SFBT provides an effective and empowering framework within which to do this. Working collaboratively, intervening only as far as is really necessary and with the aim – as I regularly tell my clients – of making ourselves, the helpers, redundant as soon as possible, tends to limit client dependency and promote independence.

A robust relationship

Over the years that I have been translating my experiences of working with clients into ideas and methodology in my training, I have increasingly found it useful to think in terms of constructing a 'robust' working relationship with clients. The first step in any helping or therapy, whatever the context, must be to engender notions of trust, safety, confidence and empathy, sufficient to enable both client and helper achieve their purpose together. I use the term 'robust' to indicate that there has to be enough strength and honesty in the relationship for both parties to act naturally and in a truly collaborative way. One cannot have a properly collaborative relationship unless both feel fully engaged and free to listen and express themselves (Bohm 1996; Lulofs and Cahn 2000). For example, and speaking personally, there is quite a lot of humour in my sessions with clients, but this can only surface naturally when the relationship will support it.

Equally, when clients have spoken to others at length such as counsellors and helpers as well as friends and family, some will have built up a 'story' and beliefs that, in effect, support their 'problem' whatever it is. With some clients it is possible to develop complicity which prevents us from asking questions that need to be asked (Boszormenyi-Nagy and Framo 1965; Watzlawick and Weakland 1977).

In effect, it doesn't feel safe or respectful to ask about certain things. This then means we are not able or willing to do our job because we enter into a 'deal' with the clients not to explore things that need discussing. In a robust relationship such barriers are not an obstacle; the relationship is safe and flexible and the client trusts the relationship enough to understand that, if the helper appears to ask 'awkward' or challenging questions, they are just doing their job. Equally, and perhaps more importantly, the helper knows that asking sensitive questions will not endanger the helper/client relationship.

Finally, and this comes more from my work in situations where there is either a high level of conflict, as in conflict resolution or anger management, or the potential for it, as with 'involuntary' clients, tensions that may arise as a result of an intervention may cause turbulence or even alienation of one or more parties, as when working with couples or families for example (Jacobson and Christensen 1996) or in child protection (Turnell and Edwards 1999). Sometimes these tensions need to be expressed and accepted or worked through. In such cases, where the relationship strays into troubled waters, it must be robust enough to weather the storm.

The therapeutic alliance

Underpinning this is the 'therapeutic alliance', well known to counsellors and other talking therapists (Frank and Frank 1991; Schaap *et al.* 1993; Wampold 2001), and one of the aspects common to all forms of therapy. It is generally recognised as one of the most important factors determining therapeutic outcome (Frank and Frank 1991; Rogers 1967; Wampold 2001).

Wampold says: 'Examination of a single common factor, the working alliance, convincingly demonstrated that this factor is a key component of psychotherapy. The alliance appears to be a necessary aspect of therapy, regardless of the nature of the therapy' (2001, p.158).

Though there is hot debate in the many different fields of helping and therapy about what this alliance is built on, there is agreement on its importance in the process of enabling people to develop the 'problem management and opportunity-developing process' (Egan 1998), which is central to the aims of therapy and helping. The therapeutic alliance is also recognised as central to helping relationships in general, not just therapy. Since writers from many other fields say that the working alliance is a key component in helping (Brammer 1999; Egan 1998; Joshi 2006; Kirsh and Tate 2006; Moore 2003), we can reasonably attribute the same importance to it in all helping settings. The term alliance implies both helper and client contributions to the process and is a strong predictor of therapeutic outcome (Metcalf *et al.* 2001). Outcome depends on the competence and motivation of the helper, the competence and motivation of the client, and the quality of the interactions (Egan 1998). A robust working relationship builds on the therapeutic alliance by ensuring equality when the practitioner genuinely treats the client as an equal partner by letting them know that their point of view provides the frame for the relationship (Street and Downey 1996).

Building rapport

Establishing a robust relationship naturally leads to questions about how to do it. Building rapport is, again, one of the givens of working effectively with others. Rapport implies that the people in a relationship are in harmony with each other, one might say on the same wavelength, have a shared perspective, feel mutually understanding of each other, and understood. As we are a social species humans have naturally evolved with the largely unconscious skills of quickly checking out whether we feel safe with another person and can trust them, and subsequently strengthening the bond, or not, by the way we interact with them. We therefore all possess these skills to some degree,[1] and they can be consciously developed further (Battino 2006; Richardson 1987). Whereas in many of our social and professional relationships we may have plenty of time to do this – it happens more or less naturally as a result of socialising or working with someone – in a helping relationship we are usually time limited and so we need to know how to actively build rapport quickly.

Though I have said that this is taken as a given in the helping professions (Walter and Peller 1992), and understanding rapport-building was a cornerstone of my own professional development, I have worked with many professionals in training who apparently have not been expressly taught how to go about it. Whatever your situation, and some people are more natural rapport-builders than others, I always say that the best description I know of this is Battino and South's *Ericksonian Approaches* (1999), which has a comprehensive chapter entitled Rapport Building Skills.

Essentially, conscious rapport-building rests on the idea that we all like people who we perceive to be like ourselves. Giving the client the sense that we understand where they are coming from, are non-judgemental, accepting and empathetic is something we can all do at a conscious level, and which therapists and helping professionals are generally trained in. Being congruent, empathetic and showing unconditional positive regard have long been seen as the necessary preconditions to therapeutic learning and change (Rogers 1967). Rapport-building refers to doing more by focusing our undivided attention on the client and giving them the sense that we are 'there for them'. We communicate this both verbally and non-verbally by what is known as pacing (Battino and South 1999; Walter and Peller 1992). In practice this means subtly mirroring (not mimicking) the client's body language, mannerisms, rate of speech including rhythm, pitch and volume, and using the client's style of language and vocabulary (Richardson 1988). 'These are ways of fitting into the client's world so that they have the sense that you understand where they come from and who they are. That is, what it is like being in their world. There needs to be a sense of collaboration, that is: *we* are in this *together*, and together we can develop ways of helping you' (Battino 2006, p.34, emphasis in original).

---

1   Some people do not, because of developmental difficulties; people on the autistic spectrum, for example.

The authors above and Richardson (1988) who I have drawn on here, acknowledge that some people are uncomfortable with the idea of consciously choosing to influence their clients. Some go further and use the word 'manipulation'. This question comes up in my workshops as well on occasion. My response is that since we cannot help but influence clients in our sessions – we cannot *not* influence (Battino and South 1999; Watzlawick 1978) – we should choose to do it to the advantage of the client. After all, the client is in the relationship to derive benefit and will make their own decisions about whether we are to be trusted or not, and the degree to which they choose to comply. As far as manipulation goes, though for some people this has a loaded meaning, I do not make those pejorative associations:

> If by manipulation you mean the unfair taking advantage of another person by devious or insidious means, the unscrupulous depriving another human being of something precious or valuable for one's own self-indulgent, inconsiderate purposes, then of course we deny and deplore it.
>
> But if by manipulation you mean the skilful use of the communicative and persuasive arts, the dextrous employment of language and diction, the judicious handling of other people's prejudices and predilections, so that the outcome of our dealings with others is mutually rewarding and productive – then we must answer yes. This is manipulation in the very best sense of the term. (Richardson 1988 pp.9–10).

My further comment is that if you are uncomfortable with the idea of consciously choosing to build rapport, then don't do it. You'll be doing it unconsciously anyway, it'll just take a little longer. Besides, as we have seen, the therapeutic alliance rests on sincerity, congruence and trust, and if rapport-building ideas are used in the service of pernicious ends as in the first paragraph above, that would breach the ethics of all therapeutic relationships, SFBT included, and an alliance would not result.

SFBT as a conversation

The task facing both helper and client is to make these interactions purposeful and effective (de Shazer *et al.* 1986), and to develop a collaborative relationship within which healing or helping conversations can take place. SFBT provides a framework for this by 'hosting therapeutic conversations', as Furman and Ahola put it (1992). The conversational style of solution-talk 'is achieved by thinking positively and by focusing on subjects that foster, such as resources, progress and the future.' (1992, p.xxiv).

Is there any situation where the solution focused approach should not be used? This is a question regularly asked during my workshops. Sometimes this is prompted by a fear that 'This would never work with *my* clients.' For others, used to prescriptive training that includes contra-indications and limitations of working with clients with certain complaints or vulnerabilities, it is a natural note of caution. I respond by saying that I do not think so. Even so, if you need to reassure yourself of this a glance through a few of the SFBT books and workshops on offer should help. A quick tour reveals authoritative SFBT practitioners in every field imaginable in social health and welfare, and increasingly in business and coaching.

Since all helpers speak to those they help and support, we are all in a position to use those conversations constructively and in a way that inspires and empowers our clients, regardless of the setting or the circumstances of the client.

I mention this because SFBT skills can be used anywhere, and with anyone capable of holding a conversation. Personally I have never found a limitation to this and I cannot think of a situation where SF ideas would be contra-indicated. There are plenty of situations or moments in a session when I might choose not to use them, but these would be moments when it would be inappropriate to do anything intended to be therapeutic anyway. For example, listening to someone who needs to tell their story, or someone who is highly distressed. Since SFBT encourages us to meet the client in their world, and to progress at a pace which is appropriate to them, I don't think there are any limitations beyond those dictated by humane sensitivity and common sense. As an extreme example, I was once working with a woman suffering from a degenerative illness and her husband. They had been having communication difficulties, she seemed to have angry outbursts and he was finding it increasingly difficult to be patient with her. She was bedridden, incapable of speaking and partially paralysed, yet we were able to communicate 'yes' and 'no' answers by the squeeze of her hand on mine, and with the help of her husband who could 'translate' and ask her to confirm certain points. My questions about what they wanted from the sessions, scaling and conversational gizmos such as reframing (her anger as natural frustration with her condition, his impatience as fuelled by worry and sadness) and normalising (most cared for/carer relationships go through difficult passages), were well received and they both reported (via scaling) improved communications and lower levels of stress. This does not mean that they were suddenly happy with their situation, their tragedy was still a tragedy, but I hope they were better able to face her decline together as a result of the improvements they reported.

Viewing SFBT sessions as conversations takes us away from traditional concepts of therapy as healing or curing, with its attendant interpretations of the therapist somehow operating on the client (de Shazer 1994). The notion of conversation brings with it suggestions of equality and openness much better suited to a collaborative helper/client relationship (Furman and Ahola 1992), more likely to produce shared understanding and consequently to be experienced by the client as supportive and helpful (Brammer and MacDonald 1999). 'We like to think of solution-talk as not a system of therapy… but as a quality of conversation. Respect, optimism, kindness and humour are not private property – they belong to everyone' (Furman and Ahola 1992, p.168).

Client motivation

Clients become clients for many reasons. Some are voluntary, seeking help with something that is troubling them. In other cases they seek help at someone else's suggestion, not entirely convinced that they can find relief, but either through urgency of the other's entreaties or threats ('Get help or I'll leave you'; 'Get help or your job will be at risk'), they turn up anyway. It follows that clients do not all share the same level of motivation when they start to work with us.

Others have no wish to seek help, but are compelled to do so by a court or some other agency. For example, I used to work with pupils in a school for young people with emotional and behavioural difficulties. I was asked to see pupils by the school on the basis that they had 'anger management problems'. As you can imagine they were not initially enthusiastic about working with me.

At the outset most of them were not really clients at all and engaging with them was difficult. Some were silent, others were rebellious or defiant, few were compliant and willing to work with me. Yet I had to engage and work with them, and this I did by 'working with what was in the room', accepting them as they were and proceeding at their pace by discussing things that were important to them, rather than pushing on with my own agenda (or the school's), to get them to deal with their 'anger problems'.

A unique facet of SFBT is the ranking devised by Steve de Shazer (1988) to distinguish clients' differing levels of engagement. He referred to Customer, Complainant and Visitor to distinguish different kinds of therapist/client relationship. It is important to note that these are not labels to be attached to particular types of client; they refer to the relationship between client and helper or therapist. Implicit in this is that the therapist can identify how they engage with clients in a way that is appropriate to the client's view.

It also reminds us that in the case of recalcitrant or uncooperative behaviour on the part of the client the onus is on the therapist or helper to do something about it, rather than writing the client off as 'resistant' or 'uncooperative'.

It is assumed that, when a client seeks help, they will voluntarily engage in the relationship with their therapist or helper, but this is not automatically the case, nor that, even when they do, their view of their situation disposes them to fully participating in the search for solutions. Making a distinction between Customer, Complainant and Visitor relationships enables the helper to understand the client's level of motivation, and to pace it. Structuring conversations like this, and using questions that encourage the client realistically and respectfully, helps them to consider the options available and matches their level of readiness and expectation (Hawkes, Marsh and Wilgosh 1998).

Customer relationship
Here the client acknowledges that they have a problem and they want help with it. They are willing to engage with the helper to tackle the problem.

'I have difficulty with my relationship/anger/depression/sleeping, etc., and I'd like to do something about it.'

This is what we are trained for! Working with people who agree that there is a problem and are willing to do something about it is relatively straightforward. The client knows what they want to work on and will do so in collaboration with the helper.

Complainant relationship
A complainant relationship is where the client accepts that there is a problem, but thinks that it is someone else's job to fix it.

'There is a problem in our relationship and if he/she would change it would be OK.'

'Of course I get angry, if he/she would only (change), my anger wouldn't be a problem.'

Here the client believes that the problem lies with someone else, their partner or manager for example. Consequently, while acknowledging that change is desirable, they see it as someone else's responsibility to make it happen. They do not see the resolution of the problem as being within their control.

The aim with this sort of relationship is to help move it towards becoming a customer relationship. My approach in such situations is to ask the client questions which will start to reflect on what they appear to be saying (there is a problem, it inconveniences me, but I have no influence so someone else must fix it).

Client: There is a problem in our relationship and if he/she would change it would be OK.

Therapist: Since he/she is not here, how realistic is it to expect them to change?

Or

Therapist: How likely do you think they are to change because we are discussing it?

Client: Not very likely, I suppose.

Therapist: So, is there anything we could do to help find a solution to the problem while you are waiting?

Rather than arguing with the client or trying to persuade them to take responsibility for something they don't see as their problem it is more constructive to engage them in a parallel discussion. For example:

- Ask them about change they would like to see happen.

- Ask them about times when the desired change, or some aspect of it, has already happened.

- Ask them how they manage to create those exceptions to the problem.

- Suggest (as a task) that between now and the next session they notice when these problem-free times occur, and reflect on how they might have contributed.

In subsequent sessions, once they have reported on the problem-free times they have noticed, get them to do more of the same.

If the client persists in saying that problem-free times are due to chance and that they have nothing to do with them, it would be useful to expand the questions more generally. For example, with a man who insisted that his wife was responsible for his bad moods I enquired about what other of his moods his wife controlled, joy? hope? ambition?... The penny finally dropped when he suddenly sat up and asked 'Are you saying that *I* am in control of my anger?' He looked genuinely amazed. We were then able to have a conversation about how people learn to control their emotions and, jokingly, how he could wrest responsibility for his moods back from his wife.

Visitor relationship

The 'client' insists that there is no problem and are unwilling to do anything about it. They may only be in therapy/helping because they have been forced to be (for example by a court or probation service). When asked 'What brings you here?':

'I don't have a problem, I'm here because I was told to come.'

'My wife/social worker/probation officer told me to come or I'd be in trouble.'

If, when asked whether there is a problem they would like help with, they say that they don't think they have a problem, I would switch to what they expected to happen in coming. For example, did they expect to sit in silence? Did they hope for a miracle?

I use probing questions to understand something of their world view, and gradually a picture will emerge. By the way, if they do respond to the question above about hoping for a miracle, I would immediately ask them a briefer version of the Miracle Question:

'And if a miracle happened, what would be different?'

When in a Visitor relationship I will work to build rapport and find something we can work on together. The aim of SFBT is to bring about change that the client wants, so *any* change will do to start the ball rolling and build trust and confidence into the relationship. From there the client might start to progress to a Complainant or Customer relationship. For example, I once worked with a 12-year-old boy, brought along by his mother, who said that he kept walking out of school during breaks 'because of bullying'. When I met the boy, without his mother, he was adamant that there was no bullying and that he was leaving school 'because he was bored'. He did not want to discuss school nor his attendance. I asked, since we had planned 'a few' sessions together, how we should spend the time? He had no idea, he said. So I asked what he did in his spare time, and was there anything he'd like to be better at, like a skill or a hobby. I told him that I sometimes help people improve at things they want to be better at. He said he'd like to be better at playing the saxophone. We discussed how he might do this and spent the rest of the time mulling over possibilities, and concluded the session with 'noticing what was better' until the next session.

I also asked him, as his mother was worried about him leaving school without permission, what we might do to stop her worrying. He said that he could agree to stay in school. I asked how he would cope with the 'boredom'. This prompted suggestions about three things he could do if he started to feel 'bored': go to the music room; go to the library; talk to a teacher. I told him that at the next session we'd work out some goals.

On his return he had not absconded from school, had started to play the saxophone more and was spending more time with his friends. I congratulated him on tackling his 'boredom' so creatively, and suggested we keep an eye on it. We concluded after the third session as he said he no longer needed to see me, and his mother confirmed that the 'problem' had disappeared.

Being in a Visitor relationship is possibly the most challenging situation helpers and therapists can find themselves involved in. Here again, the aim is at least to find a basis for discussion in the hope of building rapport and establishing enough trust to start more productive conversations. If the 'goal' is someone else's, for example, to change a drug habit or change behaviour in a way the 'client' doesn't see the need for, then it is useful to create an alternative goal with them. If the client steadfastly maintains that there is nothing they want to change, then it would be disrespectful to both them and the therapist that they attend sessions.

Thinking of how we pitch the interaction with our clients in this way is useful in that it prevents us from attempting to go too fast for the client (Hawkes *et al.* 1998). If the client does not believe that there is a problem, for example (Visitor relationship), then we won't be able to agree goals and outcomes with them. The overall aim with Complainants and Visitors is to engage them in some way until such time a 'problem' can be negotiated in order to be worked on. If, because of the setting, helper and client must continue to meet even though no collaboration is possible, then the helper should at least negotiate with the 'client' how they are going to spend the time. There is always something useful to work on, even if it is only the relationship.

Some approaches to therapy talk of clients who appear to be unable or unwilling to engage in therapy as 'resistant'. This is problematic not just because the therapist or helper is defining the client and subsequently labelling them on the basis of their perceived behaviour. It also sets the client at odds with the therapist by creating a notion of separation; the therapist is driving for therapeutic change but the client is opposing this by resisting.

SFBT takes the view that 'resistance' is a phenomenon of the relationship, rather than a characteristic of the client; it is not a question of either resisting or cooperating, but of different levels of cooperation. This assumes that all clients are doing the best they can, even if their cooperation is not immediately apparent. It is the therapist's job, first, to identify how this cooperation might be described, and second, to engage with the client by paying attention to the cooperative elements of the relationship and building on those aspects (de Shazer 1984; O'Hanlon and Weiner-Davis 1989). Rather than seeing 'resistance' it is more useful to view apparently uncooperative behaviour as an indication that something needs to be done about the client/helper relationship in order to engage with the client more fully (de Shazer 1984).

Motivation of the helper

Just as the therapeutic relationship is multi-faceted, and clients are clients for many reasons, so helpers are drawn to their professions for many reasons and motivated by many different influences. Some of the 'givens' of helping are an awareness of self and our values, a strong ethical sense, altruism and compassion, the ability to inspire and motivate others, empathy and a high degree of self-awareness, for example (Brammer and MacDonald 1999; Frank and Frank 1991).

It is for each of us to understand these motivations and to work constantly to keep them alive. But in today's increasingly pressured working environment – not to mention the demands of our own lives away from work – helpers can easily become demotivated due to constant demand and overwork (Maslach and Jackson 1981; Rafi, Oskouie and Mansoure 2004).

One of the great benefits of working in a solution focused way is that it provides a framework that keeps practitioners not just focused, but also motivated. Doing solution-talk provides an interesting starting point that helps us to remain curious about our client's resiliency, and this tends automatically to cast us in the role of enquirer, rather than fixer. There is also evidence that SFBT practitioners are less likely to suffer burnout than others in the helping professions (Thorana and Frank 2007).

This in turn enables us to draw on our own inner resources as we listen intently to our clients for exceptions and other evidence of resources that might be used in the construction of solutions. Being solution focused automatically means being motivated and helps avoid some of the stresses and pressures that can arise when helpers are required to spend time in intense involvement with other people, or working with troubled or uncooperative clients (Maslach and Jackson 1981), and so also reduces the risk of burnout.

Enhancing and empowering

Engaging in solution focused conversations to co-create solutions and define goals is, in itself, empowering for both clients and helpers. Working according to the basic assumptions of SFBT, remaining vigilant for small change, and amplifying it in order to encourage the client to do more of what is working will, if nothing else happens, nudge the client in the direction they want to go. We can be confident and sure about this on the basis of two aspects of SFBT: change is happening all the time, and small change leads to larger change.

But there is something more that therapists and helpers need to do to enhance the process. We have already seen the importance of encouragement, and it is useful to say a few words about this facet of SFBT which uses various forms of positive feedback. As well as offering encouragement, feedback empowers the client by linking positive change to their efforts. By creating a sense of agency – or co-creating with clients that what seems out of control to them is in fact within their control – is not only empowering for them, it is also likely to render our interventions more effective (O'Hanlon and Weiner-Davis 1989; Walter and Peller 1992).

Link change to client actions

Asking questions in response to news of change, or exceptions, can lead the client to make links between events they might have written off as chance encounters, and their actions. 'How did you do that?' implies that they somehow brought the change about.

Some therapists will add what is known in SF circles as cheerleading (Walter and Peller 1992):

Therapist: Is that right? You made it into work on time every day this week?

Client: Well, yes. It was a struggle though.

Therapist: That's brilliant! How did you manage that? (*Upbeat message, attributing success to client's actions*)

Client: My Mum kept shouting up the stairs for me to get up. (*Not me that did it, it was Mum*)

Therapist: And *you* did it! Just like you planned. How did you manage to turn those good intentions into actions? (*Reaffirming the view that the client made it happen*)

Client: I'm not sure, I suppose it was no fun getting into trouble for being late. (*Tacitly accepting the link*)

Therapist: Congratulations! (*upping the enthusiasm*). It sounds like you have been making some important decisions, like you want to be more popular at work.

Client: I guess I have, I mean, people are being nicer to me at work. (*Noticing more positive change linked to getting to work on time*)

The therapist uses their constant curiosity and enthusiasm to first enquire about change and then to link it to the client's actions.

Cheerleading embeds messages of personal agency and control by asking questions like:

'How did you make that happen?'

'What made you decide to do that?'

Compliments

Compliments are used to acknowledge that there are a number of things going well in the midst of the client's difficulties. They validate what clients are already doing well, and encourage change, acknowledge their problems and at the same time send a message that the therapist has been listening, understands and cares (Dolan 2010). Compliments are an integral part of SF conversations used to highlight the many small successes, positive choices, best intentions and even failed attempts by the client to address their situation (Berg and Dolan 2001). Practitioners make sincere observations based on things they have observed in the client's story or behaviour in order to 'amplify their attempted solutions and their strengths' (Hawkes *et al.* 1998). Compliments are another way of reframing things as the result of the client's actions or choices they have made (which is also an action). SF practitioners take every opportunity to highlight positive trends and comment on them, or to reframe others in a way the client had not thought of.

Compliments take different forms, for example:

Normalising: 'I am really impressed by the way you are handling a difficult situation. Divorce is never easy, and I know it has been difficult for you, yet you keep coming up with ways of reducing your stress and looking after yourself.'

Reframing: 'It shows real strength of character the way you have chosen not to blame your (alcoholic) mother for your own difficult relationship with drink. Some people would have used it as an excuse, you haven't done that. In fact you've used it as a resource by saying "I don't want to be like her".'

Compliments are seen as interventions in themselves and, as with all other interventions, it pays to be subtle and make sure they are appropriate. They work because the helper manages to present them in a way that is acceptable to the client, and fits within their view. A compliment may be presented at any time during a conversation, as long as it is low key and seems natural at that point, and is always included in the message or summary at the end of the session. They may be direct:

'I really like the way you went about that.'

'It takes courage to make the changes you have started to make, so well done!'

Or indirect:

'You have really worked at this, not many people would have put in the effort you have.'

'It shows real persistence and commitment to be able to take up your studies again.'

Sensitivity and timing are therefore all important. Simply 'bombing' the client with upbeat messages which they do not feel comfortable about will have the opposite effect and demonstrate that the helper is not in tune with them.

Predict that progress will be erratic

When clients begin to make progress it can be daunting for them to learn that progress is not even or constant. It is useful to predict this by discussing it with the client along the lines of:

> 'People sometimes notice that progress can be a little up and down. While things generally move forward, and people often are surprised at the early changes they notice (spot the presupposition), they sometimes get a little impatient. How do you think we might prepare for that?' (Collaboratively preparing for the inevitable)
>
> 'We say that progress is sometimes two steps forward and one step back. That 'one step back' might seem like more of a setback than it really is. What do you think about that?' (This is really a rhetorical question. The client's answer is less important than having have them hear the question)

It may seem counter-intuitive, when using an approach that is based on predicting success, that I should talk about setbacks. Just as it is crucial to match the client's expectations, it is also vitally important for the credibility of the practitioner that we do not overstate our belief that things will turn out well. Notwithstanding a positive, solution-oriented stance, the reality is that, even when things are going ahead and the client is clearly moving towards their goals, some days will be better than others; as clients move out of depression they have the odd bad day; chronic pain that has become more manageable returns with a vengeance for a few hours; and the arguing couple who are learning live together more harmoniously suddenly have a huge fight over some triviality. Things go up and down, and life, with all its vagaries, continues to happen.

Acknowledging and in some cases even predicting that clients might have a bad day is simply being realistic. If and when they do, it'll be no surprise to them and they'll be better prepared to deal with it. I think that this is so important there is one question that I almost always ask clients before they leave at the end of the final session, and sometimes sooner: 'What could go wrong?' This is not to predict disaster, it is to help the client think ahead and do a quick reality check before setting off to get on with their lives. The idea is to get them to do a quick mental check of possible setbacks:

'Well, I suppose we could start arguing when we are doing the shopping because we get stressed.'

'I might get a disappointing phone call, find out I haven't got the job I'm after. I might need a drink then.'

'I could start to feel that low mood descending on me again.'

At which time the helper then asks questions designed to help them prepare for what may or may not happen:

Therapist: And if you started to notice that happening, what could you do?

Client: We could agree now that if that happens we'll separate for 30 minutes or so until we've cooled off.

Client: If I get a phone call like that I could visit a neighbour to talk about it.

Client: If I feel that mood coming on I can go and see my mother, she always cheers me up.

In this way the client is prepared if an emergency occurs, they have had the opportunity to discuss it, and they have also understood that ups and downs happen, but that a down doesn't mean the end of their progress (O'Hanlon and Beadle 1994).

How far is far enough?

Small change generates bigger change and it is only necessary to start the ball rolling. People often use the same attempted solution for different problems. For example, we often have a limited range of responses to threat or conflict (Pruitt and Rubin 1993; Satir 1988), and in many situations this will be problematic. Someone who can only respond to a threat by shouting and acting aggressively would benefit from a small change, like learning to stop and think before reacting. Similarly, someone whose response is to avoid conflict at all costs might make a small change of acting more assertively in some situations. Such small changes will ripple out and have further reaching effects than the initial small change would suggest (Walter and Peller 1992; Watzlawick *et al.* 1974). This does not only apply to conflict. Since people often use the same attempted solution for all problems, by making a small change to one attempted solution 'clients can change in several situations simultaneously' (Walter and Peller 1992, p.18).

We should not assume that major change is needed to satisfy the client. Once we have helped them start the process and they begin to notice the green shoots of positive change, they will be in a more resourceful state to tackle larger problems. Noticing that they are managing some things on their own, perhaps they can continue without our help, or with less frequent sessions. In keeping with the SFBT concepts of parsimony – intervening as little as possible in the client's life – and that small change generates larger change, we should be alert for evidence of change and opportunities for the client to begin to 'go it alone' (Burwell and Chen 2006).

In preparation for this, when discussing desired change or goals with clients it is important to ask about 'first signs'; indicators that small change is happening, to increase the chances that they'll recognise it when it does:

'What will be the first sign or indication that things have begun to move in the right direction?'

'What little thing will let you know that change might be imminent?'

'What will you notice happening that'll make you more optimistic about "X"?'

Asking the client about how they will know when they don't need us any more does a number of things. It:

- presupposes that the day will come when they can manage on their own

- demonstrates the helper's belief that they will improve

- asks them to focus on what the indicators might be that they can manage alone

- reduces the likelihood of dependence

- indicates that the relationship will be of short duration (why else would we be asking such a question?).

Setting goals is fine, but people can get frustrated by waiting for the problem to be 'solved', when in reality, things rarely change at a stroke. Helping clients to become alert to small changes as they happen can help to inspire them, and also provide evidence that something is working, in which case they can do more of it (Bertolino 2003; O'Hanlon and Weiner-Davis 1989). Once things have begun to change, 'How far is far enough?' becomes the all-important question. Once we have started the ball rolling, the client can continue the momentum by themselves. However, neither they nor we will know how far is far enough unless we ask:

Client: (*complaining of difficulty sleeping*) I'd like to get a decent night's sleep. I lie awake all night then drop off just when it is time to get up.

Therapist: (*following initial information gathering, etc.*) What will you notice happening that'll make you more optimistic about getting a decent night's sleep?

Client: I'd feel more relaxed about actually going to bed, instead of all tensed up because I think I won't sleep.

Therapist: And how will you notice that you are beginning to feel more relaxed at bedtime?

Client: I guess I'll be able to concentrate on the book I'm reading.

Therapist: So when you notice yourself absorbed in your bedtime reading, you'll start to be more optimistic that your sleep might improve?

Client: Yes.

Therapist: When your sleeping habits have begun to change, how will you know you have reached a point where we no longer need to work together?

Client: If I can drop off before 1.00 am for a couple of nights a week, that would be a big improvement. I guess I could manage from there on.

This is not to suggest that these few lines of dialogue represent a whole session, I have truncated it here for illustration. The key point to remember is that clients are more likely to notice and be able to report on change if we have helped them anticipate that it will happen and what it will look like when it does.

Relationship and outcome

In this section I have looked at the helping relationship, and how it is unavoidably linked to outcome. What emerges is the close fit between helping and SFBT. The alliance between helper and client is central to the attainment of successful outcomes in therapy and helping. It is one of the core contributors to client improvement and, regardless of the style or techniques of the practitioner, it is a vital precondition of the healing process (Maione and Chenail 2001). Closely allied to this is the mindset of the practitioner, by which I mean the constellation of beliefs and attitudes towards their work and their clients. These govern how the client engages in the relationship, how well and how quickly they progress, and even how long they stay in the helping relationship (Frank and Frank 1991). Added to this the distinction of SFBT practitioners is their spirit of curiosity, enthusiasm and unshakeable belief in the human resourcefulness of their clients, coupled with self-awareness and a commitment to their own growth and learning. Conveniently, this is also the mindset of helpers in general:

> 'A general dictum among people helpers says that if I want to become more effective I must begin with myself; our personalities are thus the principal tool for the helping process.' (Brammer and MacDonald 1999, p.36)

> 'The best helpers are active in the helping sessions. They keep looking for ways to enter the worlds of their clients, to get them to become more active in their sessions, to get them to own more of it, to help them see the need for action... Although they don't push reluctant clients too hard, thus turning reluctance into resistance, neither do they sit around waiting for reluctant clients to act.' (Egan 1998, p.329).

The personal qualities of the helper are as significant for the positive growth of the client as the methods they use, and adopting a solution focused ethos means that practitioners can actively engage with their clients purposefully, effectively and confident of outcome. But this comes with two notes of caution. To be an effective SFBT practitioner places the onus on the practitioner; good progress in the client, or lack of it, is the responsibility of the helper. That is what the job is about. This means that in the case of setbacks or no progress, when seeking to remedy the situation, the practitioner must look to themselves and the helping relationship as much as to the client. It is all too common to hear of client problems that are coped with and managed, but not solved (Egan 1998), yet it is the aim of helping to collaborate with clients to find solutions. A helper or therapist who is not enabling the client to change in their chosen direction must be brave enough to question themselves to see how they can do something different.

The second caution relates to what I would call SFBT evangelism. Over the years I have met a number of people who were so enthusiastic about SFBT that in spreading the message they put others off. In one organisation I visited staff had been told by their newly SFBT enamoured boss to embrace solution focused thinking and immediately start asking all their clients the Miracle Question. Though this was undoubtedly well intentioned it was also counter-productive and damaging. As they initially received no training in or explanation of SFBT, staff completely rejected this as a fad and refused to have anything to do with it. I was subsequently asked to run a series of workshops and at each of these sessions I first had to undo the damage by winning the hearts and minds of the disaffected staff. The mere mention of solution focused approach was an immediate turn-off.

Another example was the counsellor I met who overzealously promoted SFBT in the agency where he worked. Colleagues had come to see him as some sort of heretic in their midst because the ideas he was promoting – as they saw it fewer sessions and quick fixes – conflicted with their person-centred principles. 'There's nothing worse than a convert', as they say. We have all come across people swept up in their latest passion or pastime who put us off rather than win us over to their point of view. Paradoxically, when people really understand their subject they tend to talk less about it (though some write books). This counsellor was undoubtedly committed to learning and applying SF ideas for the benefit of his clients, but his naïve over-promotion of them alienated his co-workers and probably ensured that it would be a long time before they would give SFBT any consideration. Had he really understood the principles he was promoting he would have seen that his colleagues and he were in a Visitor relationship; they were not ready to engage with him to learn more about his ideas.

These two notes of caution aside, as I have shown in this chapter, SF ideas and gizmos can easily and fruitfully be incorporated into any way of working, anywhere, in fact, where two people are having a conversation about wanting to change something. While major change can happen unexpectedly and quickly, the best approach is to aim for small change.

So here is another paradox. It is that SF practitioners are confident in what they do, have an unstinting belief in their clients' abilities, and are energetic and enthusiastic in helping them identify solutions and achieve their goals, yet they keep it quiet, confident that there are always more solutions than there are problems.

Conclusion

Starting again

I hope I have captured the spirit of Solution Focused Brief Therapy (SFBT) and the ideas the approach employs. Helping and therapy are about change, and while settings and core purposes of the various forms of helping may vary, the focus of attention to the client's needs and wishes, and enabling them to make the desired adjustments in their perceptions and responses, are common to all. SFBT is one of the most popular and widely used approaches in the world, used in therapy and a wide variety of other settings (de Shazer *et al.* 2007). I have described how it can be applied and included suggestions for practice. Now comes the action, and like all systemic approaches, the best way to develop your SFBT skills is to adopt a 'learning by doing' approach, by rolling up your sleeves and getting on with it.

I have found over the years that I have been working with students and practitioners in applying these ideas that there is really no substitute for gaining confidence through practising the techniques. As you become comfortable with them they will develop into habits which will be woven into your conversations with clients and others. 'Once the basic assumptions and the way of thinking are mastered, the technique becomes less important than the relationship with the client' (Hawkes *et al.* 1998, p.12). Like anything new this will feel strange. The more so because SFBT requires us to abandon preconceived and inherited ideas about therapeutic change and interactions and embrace something new.

Some people find learning how to do solution-talk more difficult than others, and those who are already 'married' to another belief system tend to find it more challenging to make the shift (Berg and Miller 1992). The good news is that adopting these ideas doesn't require abandoning anything (nor divorce), simply put your existing framework to one side and open your mind to possibilities…

A new framework

SFBT is not context-bound, it can be used in all settings. In my workshops and training I have always encouraged people to introduce some of the facets of SFBT into their work and see what happens. I don't believe that it is necessarily useful or helpful to try to persuade practitioners who are coming to SFBT for the first time and may be cautious about trying something new that it has to be adopted wholesale for it to be effective.

Anyone can use the Miracle Question to see where it takes the conversation. Likewise, scaling, reframing, normalising and setting tasks are things that are common practice in many different fields, so many people in the helping professions are familiar with them already. Combining these techniques into the framework outlined here will help you become more accustomed to thinking about clients and their problems from an SF perspective. In order to really benefit, of course, there has to be a shift to genuinely understanding and doing SF thinking.

In my experience, this is a developmental process. Some people are completely enamoured with SFBT from their first introduction to it, others take a little more time to be convinced. In either case, it generally takes some time and practice for people to really 'get' thinking in an SF way. The essential simplicity of the approach often escapes people who have been trained to think in terms of complexity and analysis, to shift from breaking things down to 'snapshots' to seeing things in terms of an interrelated whole. It is a framework that focuses on relationships between things rather than the things themselves (Senge 2006).

If we choose to look for complexity in the problems our clients bring us we will surely find it. On the other hand, if we choose to look for a simpler alternative, speaking our clients' language and believing them to be resourceful enough to move forward with as little help as possible, we can be amazed by the results. I have also described SFBT as like learning a new language, only simpler. That language is solution-talk, and it can happen in any setting where a conversation is appropriate. While learning the art of conversation comes more naturally to some than to others, it is certainly something which is natural to effective helpers. Adapting to an SF way of thinking and talking is a matter of learning new habits.

Like learning anything new, the mantra is practice, practice, practice. Treat yourself as the client and follow the recommendations of SFBT: aim for small achievable goals, and remember that acknowledging your progress on a regular progress will help build confidence with these new habits. Remember that small change generates bigger change, and small successes generate greater confidence.

Social worker and trainer Fletcher Peacock, writing on solution focused communication, calls this approach the 'philosophy of cooperation'. He poses five basic questions that we should ask ourselves:

- Do you see problems, or opportunities?

- Do you experience failures, or learnings?

- Do you live in a world where there is only one truth, or many?

- Is there only one solution, or thousands?

- Do you water the flowers, or the weeds?

In this final question, which provides the title of his book (Peacock 2001), he has chosen a metaphor which goes to the heart of SF thinking: that which we focus on becomes our reality. Our clients come to us for help, trusting that we will be good enough at our job to help them thrive. They bring with them the seeds of their own solutions. We can choose to nurture and cultivate these by building on their previous solutions and exceptions to their problems, or we can overlook them, focus on problems and causes, and keep the weeds alive.

In the next section you will find a transcript of a complete SF session. This will take you through the various steps and techniques and will, I hope, bring the preceding pages alive in a new way.

Appendix: Putting It Together

This is the transcript of a single session with a 32-year-old divorcee who called the clinic to say that she needed help with a 'problem'. She gave no further details at that time, other than her contact details.

Introduction

Therapist: Well, hi, Brenda, isn't it?

Client: Hi. Yes, Brenda.

Therapist: So, what brings you here?

Client: Um, well I mean, over the last three, four years I think I've probably had, I have just been through so many jobs I can't even begin to tell you and I think I was actually sacked from my last job which I just, it's just literally the last straw, I just, you know, I just feel that I can't, you know, that's it.

Therapist: What would you like to have happen as a result of us working together? How would things be different?

Client: I just need to keep down a job for more than three months, I need to be able to know that I can do that, and I just can't.

Therapist: So, when we've finished working together, well presumably at least three months after that, you will have held a job down?

Client: Yeah.

Therapist: And, what difference will that make to you? I mean so that I understand.

Client: Well, I'm not good on my own, I mean if I'm left to my own devices, because I'm not married I literally just spend the whole time just, I just go to pieces. I don't work. It's not just money it's... (pause)

Therapist: It makes a big impact.

Client: It makes a huge, you know, it's just... (expansive gesture with hands)... huge.

Therapist: So, a bit of a strange question but I'd like to see what you make of this. I'd like you to imagine, when you get home tonight, you go to sleep as usual and while you are asleep a miracle happens and the miracle means that the problem that brought you here has disappeared. You wake in the morning problem-free, you don't know it yet because nobody's told you the miracle's happened because you've been asleep. So what would tell you, if the thing spontaneously disappeared, you wake up in the morning, what would be different that would tell you that a miracle's just happened?

Client: (Pause) I don't need a drink when I wake up.

Therapist: So you wake up. What would you be doing? How will you know what's different about that?

Client: That I would just...that the first thing I want is breakfast.

Therapist: So you wake up hungry for breakfast?

Client: Hungry.

Therapist: OK. What else?

Client: I'll have a job to go to.

Therapist: In the interim, obviously ultimately you will, in the interim?

Client: I'll be busy.

Therapist: So you'll wake up, you'll want breakfast, you'll obviously cook your breakfast or whatever you do...

Client: Yeah, I'll have a reason to get up in the morning, even if it's not a job.

Therapist: You'll feel motivated?

Client: Yes. I'll feel inspired to get out there and do something, even if it's going swimming.

Therapist: OK. Anything else?

Client: I just wanna, you know, meet up with people and get out there.

Therapist: So more active, more motivated, more social.

Client: Yeah, get out there more.

Therapist: And what difference will these things make to you?

Client: I suppose I won't feel so lonely.

Therapist: So what will you be feeling then?

Client: In control.

Therapist: So you'll be feeling more in control and anything else? I'm not sure how control equates as an antithesis of loneliness.

Client: Well, if I'm seeing people then I'm more able to deal with things, I'm more able to have a conversation, I'm more able to have a laugh. The need to drink is less likely to take over, I feel more in control.

Therapist: (*summarising*) So then, you'll wake up, hungry, breakfast, do the breakfast, all the other stuff associated with that, you'll have something to do, you'll feel more motivated and because of those things, and you'll be seeing more people, that is actually a lifter of mood in some way.

Client: Yeah. Because it will be different.

Therapist: OK.

Client: There'll be not doing what I always do. (*Framed in the negative*)

Therapist: It will be doing what then? (*Request for her to respond in the positive*)

Client: It will be being active and going out and seeing people.

Therapist: Looking forward to going out, motivated, and in a lighter mood perhaps?

Commentary

Brenda starts with a brief description, and apparently wants help with her ability to keep a job. Her answer to the Miracle Question takes the conversation in a different direction though. Her first answer is 'I don't need a drink…'. The therapist asks for more information, as this first response is given in the negative ('I don't...'). Brenda's next few answers quickly sketch a problem-free morning where she would be hungry for breakfast and she will 'be being active and going out and seeing people'. In response to her answer 'not doing what I always do...'. Once again the therapist asks her to respond in the positive, by asking what she *will* be doing.

There followed a brief conversation about motivation, not reproduced here, in which Brenda talked about the 'lack of motivation' that had been stopping her getting on with things in the morning.

Scaling

Therapist: In relation to these feelings and sense of lack of motivation, all these things, the problems, if one is the worst you have felt and ten is where you'd like to be, well let's say nine because very few people get to ten in real life but where are you now?

Client: Three.

Therapist: Three. So you're actually two up from one.

Client: (*Laughs*)

Therapist: Yes, I know, but it shows movement can happen, doesn't it? Have you ever been lower than one?

Client: Oh yeah. I've been zero.

Therapist: So you've been at zero?

Client: Well, I've felt there, yeah.

Therapist: And yet, somehow, you've kept on getting up and getting on?

Client: Yeah.

Therapist: OK...and that has been hard, obviously.

Client: Yeah.

Therapist: So it might actually get easier, one could hope. What level, if we could get you up one or two points on the scale, let's say, to five, by this time next week, would that be an acceptable level to start knowing that something's changing?

Client: (*Startled*) In...how much time...a week?

Therapist: Mmm.

Client: What do I have to do for something to happen?

Therapist: Well, you don't have to do anything, that's the point.

Client: Right.

Therapist: What I'm wondering is, what would *have to happen* in that time? What would tell you that you'd arrived at a five?

Client: I'd have a good interview or something.

Therapist: OK, well let's say two weeks then, it would be easier wouldn't it, you've got to apply for a job, sending out your CV, all of that...

Client: Yeah.

Therapist: So, one of the things, you might have an interview?

Client: Yeah, if I got an interview and I have a good interview, even if I didn't get the job I think, there just needs to be a glimmer of hope, you know.

Therapist: OK, is there anything else that could get you up one or two points on that scale?

Client: Going to the doctor, sort out the drinking.

Therapist: So, doing something about the drink.

Client: Yeah.

Therapist: OK.

Client: Even if I had one day of not drinking, that would be huge.

Therapist: So, in practical concrete terms then, if we can organise it so that you have one day without drinking in the next week, you would have moved up on that scale.

Client: Yeah.

Therapist: You said it would be huge. How much?

Client: How much what?

Therapist: How much huge, I mean, how much up on the scale do you think you would be now?

Client: You mean to have a whole day without drinking? That would literally be, I mean, that would be six or seven for me.

Therapist: So if you had half a day, you'd be at four or five?

Client: Yeah. If I could get through the morning and not have a drink.

Therapist: And would you find, do you think, that if you did that it might be easier to get through the afternoons?

Client: Yeah, the mornings are the worst.

Therapist: I thought that, I mean people tell me that sometimes.

Commentary

Scaling provides more information. The therapist constantly, but tentatively, offers mini summaries and reinterpretations to Brenda. For example, 'three' becomes 'two up from one', demonstrating that movement has happened; 'being at zero' is fed back to the client as an indication that she has, despite the low point, 'kept on getting up and getting on'. This is acknowledged as being hard for her to do – matching Brenda's experience and so a truism – and linked to a speculation that things might improve, thus linking the truism to a suggestion. Brenda accepts these reframes, which demonstrated resourcefulness, as the conversation continues to flow.

When asked how 'we could get you up one or two points on the scale' (collaborative), Brenda seemed startled, perhaps worried about what she was going to be expected to do. 'Would have to happen' is a more ambiguous way of asking the question. Because of Brenda's apparent alarm, the therapist puts the emphasis on factors outside the client, rather than on things she would have to do. This avoids pressure on her to act before she is ready to.

One of Brenda's indicators would be to have an interview to go to. This is not realistic within a week, so the therapist suggests two weeks to give her time to apply for jobs. The therapist 'downgrades' in a similar way when the conversation turns to a 'whole day without drinking', as half a day (smaller change), is more likely to succeed than a whole day.

The therapist closes this section by normalising 'the mornings are the worst', with 'people tell me that sometimes'.

Exceptions

Therapist: I am interested to know, speaking about the drinking habit which you said earlier you felt pretty much had control of you at times, 'took you over', I think were your words, are there any times when it's less of a problem, when you feel you have control over it, for example?

Client: Er, I look after my sister's children twice a week or whenever she's busy and she goes out quite a lot and when I look after them it wouldn't occur to me because I have to be sober to make sure, because they are two, seven and eight.

Therapist: So when you're looking after the kids it just isn't an issue?

Client: No, I don't even think about it.

Therapist: Brilliant. Any other times?

Client: When I'm really busy, you know, when I'm...

Therapist: ...occupied?

Client: Yeah, when I've got to focus then I don't even think about it.

Therapist: And what about times when you have been thinking about it but you've still got control over it?

Client: It's because I know something's going to happen, it's often an hour before maybe going out, an hour before something and I've got an hour to kill and I just think, oh, I've got an hour to kill and I'm on my own and so that's...

Therapist: You've overcome it at times like that?

Client: Well, you know, I've gone out or I've, you know...

Therapist: Occupied yourself?

Client: ...had a cigarette or I've just put the TV on or I've just done the ironing or something.

Therapist: OK. So (A), looking after the kids?

Client: Yeah.

Therapist: (B), focused on the job or something else at hand?

Client: Yeah.

Therapist:	But (C), even more resourcefully, times when it could have struck, you've managed to fend it off by occupying yourself with something?
Client:	Yeah.
Therapist:	Brilliant. That's really useful information.
Client:	Yeah. I know I can do it.

Commentary

The therapist refers to the implied drink problem as a 'drinking habit', and starts to externalise it at the same time, first by giving it an identity by calling it a habit, second by picking up on Brenda's language when she said it 'took over', which suggests invasion by something external. The purpose of this part of the intervention is to identify times when Brenda felt she was in control of the problem, at least partially (exceptions).

Brenda immediately identified several examples, adding that she 'didn't even think about it.' Since she might attribute these to chance, the therapist asks her to expand on this by looking for times when she had been thinking about it but still had control over it (greater agency), and she confirmed that there are exceptions like this too. The therapist then summarises (A, B and C), indirectly compliments Brenda ('Brilliant,... useful information) and Brenda affirms that she 'knows she can do it'.

Motivation

Therapist:	Well, thanks for telling me all that. You looked like you really want to get some results in this.
Client:	I know I can't keep going on, I mean it's just reached that point now.
Therapist:	How desperate is it to get some results? Or let me ask you more specifically, how confident are you that you can do it, on a scale of one to ten?
Client:	Ten.
Therapist:	So it's really right up there?
Client:	Yeah.

Therapist: …That's a really good sign. Now, I appreciate that you wouldn't be here if you thought this was going to be easy. And I actually know from experience it needn't be too difficult, but we're going to have to work on it together, so how motivated are you, do you think, to go through some times which are…

Client: I mean, I think when you've lost as many jobs as I have in the last couple of years, there isn't any other way forward for me, I've got to do something.

Therapist: So you're being pushed rather than pulled? In other words, you're being pushed by circumstances in a way, which is pretty powerful.

Client: Yeah. Also there's no quality of life, I mean, I have got some pride.

Therapist: Of course, I can see that.

Client: And I don't want to be a figure of fun, I've already been completely ostracised by some of my family and everything and I don't want to be seen like that all my life.

Therapist: So, I come back to my question, perhaps motivation wasn't the right word, what about how confident are you that from this point on…

Client: I am confident!

Therapist: On a scale of one to ten…?

Client: (*reflectively*) Seven, eight? I am confident.

Commentary

Brenda's response to the 'confidence' scaling question seemed too quick and lacked authenticity. The therapist therefore re-posed the question by asking her to scale her level of 'motivation'. This time the answer was more considered and Brenda seemed more engaged when answering it.

Limiting beliefs

Therapist: You mentioned earlier that, this drinking question, you mentioned your mother in relation to something that happened, can you tell me a little more about that?

Client: I always remember, because both my parents are really quite eccentric and I remember, I think one of the earliest memories I have of my mum, and I didn't have any idea what was going on, we were on holiday in Italy and my parents had rented a little villa, like a flat, you know, and I remember being on the beach and the beach was completely full of tourists and Italians and people and everything, you know, and looking up and seeing my mum walking towards us from the other end of the beach and she was completely pissed, and it was the most humiliating…it's like one of the memories you never forget, you know. And I remember her stumbling and falling down and that everybody could see it and I didn't realise that she had a problem because I just thought she'd just had a bit too much to drink and I think when you're kind of brought up with that you think it's not a problem because no one actually ever says to you it's a problem, they just say she's just had a bit too much to drink, she went to a soiree, she went to a luncheon party, and then you think, well she goes to a hell of a lot of luncheon parties.

Therapist: And…

Client: So I didn't realise that…it wasn't ever really spoken about.

Therapist: So, you believe that your Mum had a drink problem.

Client: She was an alcoholic, I mean she was drunk practically every day now I remember it, she was always slurring her words and she would be fine and she would have a kind of control over it but then she'd do something that would let slip that she was drunk, but she just managed to disguise it really really well, and she'd drive, I mean, you know, she'd be driving pissed! You know and it's just… (tails off)

Therapist: …Pretty repugnant to you, the whole idea?

Client: Yeah, I mean you know, yeah, completely.

Therapist: So, what does this mean to you today, apart from obviously the discomfort and things we talked about?

Client: Yeah, I just feel, I mean that's the thing, I just feel a bit ashamed of myself that I've...because I think that I don't want to become like my mum. I don't want to become like her, I don't want to humiliate my children when I have them, I don't want to be falling down on a beach in Italy and that is the thing that gets me out of this, I just think I don't want to become like her.

Commentary

Some clients attribute difficulties to things outside their control. For example 'It runs in the family', or 'It's in the genes'. Alcohol problems, in particular, are often accompanied by disempowering beliefs of this kind. As Brenda had mentioned her mother's drinking the therapist wanted to check that this was not associated with limiting beliefs of this kind. However, and on the contrary, Brenda seems to be using recollections of her mother's drinking as a motivator.

Review and message

Therapist: If I can just check back with you because I've noticed a number of things, I just want to make sure I've fully understood. Then I think there are a couple of things you could do through the week to start the process off, and then we'll take it from there.

Client: OK.

Therapist: This has obviously been a source of great distress to you. It's not actually an overnight problem, it's been going on for a couple of years now that you've been building this sense of...

Client: Yeah.

Therapist: ...defeatist hopelessness or whatever has been going on. But despite that you've gone from a zero at your worst to a three today and that you've been very helpful in that you've helped me focus on relatively small steps to take. For example, going through a morning without drinking would actually start to nudge you up that scale fairly significantly.

You have also been really helpful in that you've given me some clear ideas, and yourself I hope, about, if a miracle could happen, what it might be like. Now, I know miracles don't happen and I wouldn't mislead you, but I have seen miraculous things happen and in a way you've had a series of mini miracles. They don't seem like it when you're there, but in the period that you've mentioned, to go from a zero to a three and then come along here and have your sight set on going up the scale a bit further, that takes courage, commitment.

I think I have also got, really strongly, something of how you feel about this. I really sense the feeling of sadness tinged with humiliation about your mother and the fact that you haven't turned that into a blame, you've actually used it as a resource to say, 'I don't want to be like that', because you know, some people would have used it as an excuse. You haven't done that, which is another thing that points to this innate sense of motivation you seem to have.

So, what I would suggest over the next week is that you look out for any positive changes as they occur, anything at all, anything in any area of your life, so that you can tell me next week, what it is you want to keep in your life. You say you want the drinking to go, but I would really like to know, for example, do you want to never drink again, or do you want to be able to drink a little socially, what do you want to keep in your life in relation to this difficulty about drinking. And then to look at the work situation, I would ask the same question, what do you want to keep in your life in relation to work, because the great thing about you which seems to escape you, is that you know how to get a job. Now, you may not know how to keep one too well at the moment, but anybody that can have as many jobs, can *get* as many jobs, as you have had in two years, and go through the job for a week or two, you're doing a lot right. Now, keeping a job is quite different from getting a job, and the question I'd like you to focus on is, how much and how long do you actually want to keep the same job?

Commentary

After a short break for reflection, the therapist summarises, first by acknowledging Brenda's difficulties and sense of helplessness etc. Brenda seems to agree, with 'Yeah', and from there the therapist outlines a number of things Brenda is already doing that are working for her, complimenting her ('You've been really helpful'), and reframing her successes as 'mini miracles', complimenting her on her commitment in struggling with a situation that she has found difficult and yet she has still had the courage to seek out help.

Despite her obvious frustration and sadness on recollection of her mother's drinking, Brenda has avoided blame and is using the experience as a resource (motivator). The therapist concludes the summary with a task, using the 'skeleton-key' questions: 'Look out for any positive changes as they occur', and 'What it is you want to keep in your life?'

The therapist also asks Brenda to consider to what degree she wants change to happen (how far is far enough?), for example to eliminate drinking entirely or to just manage it better. Finally, and finishing on an upbeat note, the therapist reframes Brenda's frequent job change scenario as both a skill (getting jobs), and a skill deficit (knowing how to keep a job).

What could go wrong?

Therapist: You've said that you are pretty confident that you can start to make those changes we've spoken about and in particular start exploring the idea of having a day free of drinking and we've discussed some of the ways you might do that, but we've said maybe let's go for half a day, a morning, to start with.

Client: OK.

Therapist: So that's your target and you said to me that you were about seven on the scale of one to ten in terms of confidence with that and that if you felt it slipping you could call your sister and talk to her and you've got a couple of things you can do. Is there anything that could go wrong, by that I mean, you're going through the week absolutely fine, getting on with things... Is there anything that could intrude, that could break that resolve or start the thing going down the slippery slope to allowing the drink to...

Client:	Only if I spent too much time on my own, I mean I think if I had a bad phone call, or I try to get an interview, didn't get an interview and then I'd be quite defeated and think oh, I'll stay at home today, I'm not going to do anything.
Therapist:	So, disappointment, then, disappointment.
Client:	Yeah, that would set me back.
Therapist:	Now, we're only talking about the next week from now on. How likely is it that you will get one of those phone calls? I mean, for example, have you actually applied for any jobs at the moment?
Client:	A couple.
Therapist:	OK, so you might do. Can we think of ways in which, let's hope it doesn't happen, but, in a worst case scenario, you're going along fine, you get a phone call, rather than just going and getting a drink…
Client:	I could pick up the phone and speak to someone else. I could pick up the phone and phone a friend, phone somebody.
Therapist:	So you could actually do that?
Client:	Yeah.
Therapist:	And have you got people who are available pretty well all the time if you needed to?
Client:	I've got a neighbour who works from home who I have gone into and had a chat with.
Therapist:	Now I'd leave this to you but that seems like a pretty good strategy. There may be some way of, without revealing too much about yourself, lining them up so that you know that you've got a resource there.
Client:	Yeah, I mean everyone's allowed to be disappointed if they don't get a job so if I just say to my neighbour, I've just had a pretty bad phone call and I didn't get this job, she's not going to think 'weirdo'.
Therapist:	So you've got plan B and that would work for you?
Client:	Yeah, it's worked in the past, it's just I don't call on people as much as I should.

Commentary

Brenda has said that she is confident to start making some small changes. She has already identified times when she can be drink-free, even when she has been tempted she has found ways of distracting herself, and has named a number of other ideas and strategies.

In real life, despite people's best intentions during the session, things can go wrong, so the therapist asks Brenda to think ahead and identify any times when her resolve could start 'slipping'. Brenda identifies some potentially risky moments, and at the therapist's prompting comes up with some strategies to keep her on the straight and narrow.

References

Anderson, H. and Goolishan, H. (1988) 'Human systems as linguistic systems: preliminary and evolving ideas about the implications for clinical theory.' *Family Process 27*, 371–393.

Bachelor, A. and Horvarth, A. (2001) 'The Therapeutic Relationship.' In M. Hubble, B. Duncan and S. Miller (eds) *The Heart and Soul of Change: What Works in Therapy.* Washington: APA.

Balint, M. and Balint E. (1961) *Psychotherapeutic Techniques in Medicine.* London: Tavistock Publications.

Barksy, A. (2000) *Conflict Resolution for the Helping Professions.* Belmont, CA: Brooks/Cole Publishing.

Battino, R. (2006) *Expectation: The Very Brief Therapy Book.* Carmarthen: Crown House Publishing.

Battino, R. and South, T. (1999) *Ericksonian Approaches: A Comprehensive Manual.* Carmarthen: Crown House Publishing.

Berg, I. and Dolan, Y. (2001) *Tales of Solutions: A Collection of Hope-Inspiring Stories.* New York: W.W. Norton.

Berg, I. and Miller, S. (1992) *Working with the Problem Drinker: A Solution Focused Approach.* New York: W.W. Norton.

Bertolino, B. (2003) *Change Oriented Therapy with Adolescents and Young Adults.* New York: W.W. Norton.

Beyebach, M., Moréjon, A.R., Palenzuela, D.L. and Rodriguez-Arias, J.L. (1996) 'Research on the Process of Solution Focused Brief Therapy.' In S. Miller, M. Hubble and B. Duncan (eds) *Handbook of Solution Focused Brief Therapy.* San Francisco, CA: Jossey-Bass.

Bliss, V. and Bray, D. (2009) 'The smallest solution focused particles: Towards a minimalist definition of when therapy is solution focused.' *Journal of Systemic Therapies 28*, 2, 62–74.

Bohm, D. (1996) *On Dialogue.* London: Routledge.

Bolletino, R.C. and Le Shan, L. (1997) 'Cancer: The Roots of Mind Body Treatment for Cancer Patients.' In A. Watkins (ed.) *Mind-Body Medicine: A Clinicians Guide to Psychoneuroimmunology.* New York: Churchill Livingstone.

Booker, C. (2004) *The Seven Basic Plots: Why We Tell Stories.* London: Continuum.

Boszormenyi-Nagy, I. and Framo, J. (1965) *Intensive Family Therapy: Theoretical and Practical Aspects.* New York: Brunner-Mazel.

Brammer, L. and MacDonald, G. (1999) *The Helping Relationship: Process and Skills.* Boston: Allyn and Bacon.

Brothers, L. (1997) *Friday's Footprint: How Society Shapes the Human Mind.* New York; Oxford University Press.

Burwell, R. and Chen, C. (2006) 'Applying the principles of solution-focused therapy to career counselling.' *Counselling Psychology Quarterly 19,* 2, 189–203.

Chaika, E. (2000) *Linguistics, Pragmatics and Psychotherapy: A Guide for Therapists.* London: Whurr Publishers.

Combs, A.W. (1971) *Helping Relationships: Basic Concepts for the Helping Professions.* Boston, MA: Allyn and Bacon.

Cooper, J. (1995) *A Primer of Brief Psychotherapy.* New York: W. W. Norton.

Cousins, N. (1983) *The Healing Heart: Antidotes to Panic and Helplessness.* New York: W. W. Norton.

de Bono, E. (1994) *Parallel Thinking.* London: Penguin.

de Shazer, S. (1984) 'The death of resistance.' *Family Process 23,* 11–17.

de Shazer, S. (1985) *Keys to Solution in Brief Therapy.* New York: W. W. Norton.

de Shazer, S. (1986) 'An Indirect Approach to Brief Therapy.' In S. de Shazer and R. Kral (eds) *Indirect Approaches to Therapy.* Rockville, MD: Aspen Publishers Inc.

de Shazer, S. (1988) *Clues: Investigating Solutions in Brief Therapy.* New York: W. W. Norton.

de Shazer, S. (1994) *Words Were Originally Magic.* New York: W. W. Norton.

de Shazer, S., Berg, I., Lipchik, E., Nunnally, E., *et al.* (1986) 'Brief therapy: Focused solution development.' *Family Process 25,* 207–221.

de Shazer, S., Dolan, Y., Korman, H., Trepper, T., McCollum, E. and Berg, I.K. (2007) *More than Miracles, the State of the Art of Solution-Focused Brief Therapy.* New York: Routledge.

DOH (2009) *Report of the Standing Commission on Carers 2007 to 2009.* London: Department of Health.

Dolan, Y. *What is Solution Focused Brief Therapy?* Highland, IN: Institute for Solution-Focused Therapy. Available at www.solutionfocused.net, accessed on 27 July 2010.

Dryden, W. and Feltham, C. (1993) *Dictionary of Counselling.* London: Whurr Publishers.

Egan, G. (1994) *The Skilled Helper: A Problem-Management Approach to Helping* (5th edition). Pacific Grove, CA: Brooks/Cole Publishing.

Egan, G. (1998) *The Skilled Helper: A Problem-Management Approach to Helping* (6th edition). Pacific Grove, CA: Brooks/Cole Publishing.

Elgin, S. (2000) *The Language Imperative.* Cambridge, MA: Perseus Books.

Evans, D. (2001) *Emotions, A Very Short Introduction.* Oxford: Oxford University Press.

Frank, J.D. and Frank, J. (1991) *Persuasion and Healing: A Comparative Study of Psychotherapy.* Baltimore: Johns Hopkins University Press.

Freedman, J. and Combs, G. (1996) *Narrative Therapy: The Social Construction of Preferred Realities.* New York: W. W. Norton.

Furman, B. and Ahola, T. (1992) *Solution Talk: Hosting Therapeutic Conversions.* London: W.W. Norton.

Gingerich, W. (2010) *What is Solution-Focused Brief Therapy?* Available at www.gingerich.net/ ISFBT, accessed on 6 August 2010.

Ginsberg, B. (1997) *Relationship Enhancement Family Therapy.* New York: John Wiley and Sons.

Glucksberg, S. (2001) *Understanding Figurative Language: From Metaphors to Idioms.* Oxford: Oxford University Press.

Goldberg, M.C. (1998) *The Art of the Question: A Guide to Short-term Question Centered Therapy.* New York: John Wiley and Sons.

Gottman, J., Notarius, C., Gonso, J. and Markman, H. (1976) *A Couple's Guide to Communication.* Champaign, IL: Research Press.

Gottman, J. (1993) *What Predicts Divorce?: The Relationship Between Marital Processes and Marital Outcomes.* Hillsdale, NJ: Laurence Earlbaum Publishers.

Gottman, J. (1999) *The Marriage Clinic: A Scientifically Based Marital Therapy.* New York: W.W. Norton.

Greenberg, R. (2001) 'Common Psychosocial Factors in Psychiatric Drug Therapy.' In M. Hubble, B. Duncan and S. Miller (eds) *The Heart and Soul of Change: What Works in Therapy.* Washington: American Psychological Association.

Haden Elgin, S. (1999) *The Language Imperative: How Learning Language Can Enrich Your Life and Expand Your Mind.* Cambridge, MA: Perseus Books.

Haley, J. (1976) *Problem Solving Therapy.* New York: Harper & Row.

Hawkes, D., Marsh, T. and Wilgosh, R. (1998) *Solution Focused Therapy: A Handbook for Health Care Professionals.* Oxford: Butterworth-Heinemann.

Hawkes, D., Marsh, I. and Wilgosh, R. (1998) *Solution-focused Therapy: A Practical Guide for Health Care Professionals.* London: Butterworth-Heinemann.

Hawkins, P. and Shohet, R. (1989) *Supervision in the Helping Professions: An Individual, Group and Organizational Approach.* Milton Keynes: Open University Press.

Hawkins, P. and Shohet, R. (2000) *Supervision in the Helping Professions.* Milton Keynes: Open University Press.

Hayakawa, S. and Hayakawa, R. (1990) *Language in Thought and Action* (5th edition) San Diego, CA: Harcourt Brace Jovanovich.

Henden, J. (2008) *Preventing Suicide: The Solution Focused Approach.* Chichester: Wiley and Sons.

Hewstone, M. (1989) *Causal Attribution: From Cognitive Processes to Collective Beliefs.* Oxford: Basil Blackwell.

Hubble, M., Duncan, B. and Miller, S. (1997) *Psychotherapy with 'Impossible' Cases.* New York: W.W. Norton.

Hubble, M., Duncan, B. and Miller, S. (eds) (2001) *The Heart and Soul of Change: What Works in Therapy.* Washington: American Psychological Association.

Jacobson, N. and Christensen, A. (1996) *Integrative Couple Therapy: Promoting Acceptance and Change.* New York: W.W. Norton.

Johnson, J.G. (1972) *General Semantics: An Outline Survey.* San Francisco, CA: International Society for General Semantics.

Johnson, W. (1946) *People in Quandaries: The Semantics of Personal Adjustment*. New York: Harper & Row.

Joshi, S. (2006) 'Teamwork: The therapeutic alliance in pediatric pharmacotherapy.' *Child and Adolescent Psychiatric Clinics of North America 15*, 1, 239–262.

Keeley, S.M. (1995) *Asking the Right Questions in Abnormal Psychology*. Englewood Cliffs, NJ: Prentice Hall.

Kirsh, B. and Tate, E. (2006) 'Developing a comprehensive understanding of the working alliance in community mental health.' *Qualitative Health Research 16*, 1054–1074.

Lakoff, G. and Johnson, M. (1980) *Metaphors We Live By*. Chicago: University of Chicago Press.

Lass, R. (1987) *The Shape of English: Structure and History*. London: J. M. Dent & Sons.

Levi, P. (1990) *Other People's Trades*. London: Sphere Books.

Lipchik, E. (2002) *Beyond Technique in Solution Focused Therapy*. New York: Guilford Press.

Lulofs, R. and Cahn, D. (2000) *Conflict: From Theory to Action*. Boston: Allyn and Bacon.

Maione, P. and Chenail, R. (2001) *Qualitative Inquiry in Psychotherapy: Research on the Common Factors*. In M. Hubble, B. Duncan and S. Miller (eds) *The Heart and Soul of Change: What Works in Therapy*. Washington: American Psychological Association.

Marinoff, L. (1999) *Plato Not Prozac: Applying Philosophy to Everyday Problems*. New York: Harper Collins.

Maslach, C. and Jackson, S. (1981) 'The measurement of experienced burnout.' *Journal of Occupational Behavior 2*, 99–113.

McKeel, A.J. (1996) *A Clinician's Guide to Research on Solution-Focused Brief Therapy*. San Francisco, CA: Jossey-Bass.

McKergow, M.W. and Korman, H. (2009) 'Inbetween – not inside or outside: The radical simplicity of solution-focused brief therapy.' *Journal of Systemic Therapies 28*, 2, 34–49.

Meichenbaum, D. (2001) *Treatment of Individuals with Anger-Control Problems and Aggressive Behaviours: A Clinical Handbook*. Clearwater, FL: Institute Press.

Metcalf, L., Thomas, F., Duncan, B., Miller, S. and Hubble, M. (2001) 'What Works in Solution-Focused Brief Therapy: A Qualitative Analysis of Client and Therapist Perceptions.' In S. Miller, M. Hubble and B. Duncan (eds) *Handbook of Solution-Focused Brief Therapy*. San Francisco, CA: Jossey-Bass.

Miller, S. Hubble, M. and Duncan, B. (eds) (1996) *Handbook of Solution Focused Brief Therapy*. San Francisco, CA: Jossey-Bass.

Miller, S., Hubble, M. and Duncan, B. (1997) 'No more bells and whistles.' *The Family Therapy Networker 19*, 2, 52–58, 62–63.

Mills, J. and Crowley, R. (1986) *Therapeutic Metaphors Children and the Child Within*. Philadelphia, PA: Brunner-Mazel Inc.

Minsky, M. (1987) *The Society of Mind*. London: Heinemann.

Moore, C. (2003) *The Mediation Process: Practical Strategies for Resolving Conflict*. San Francisco, CA: Jossey-Bass.

O'Connell, B. and Palmer, S. (2003) *Solution-Focused Therapy*. London: Sage.

O'Connell, B. (1998) *Solution-Focused Therapy.* London: Sage.

O'Hanlon, W. and Beadle, S. (1994) *A Field Guide to Possibility Land: Possibility Therapy Methods.* Omaha, NE: Possibility Press.

O'Hanlon, W. and Weiner-Davis, M. (1989) *In Search of Solutions, A New Direction in Psychotherapy.* New York: W.W. Norton.

Ogles, B., Anderson, T. and Lunnen, K. (2001) *The Contribution of Models and Techniques to Therapeutic Efficacy.* In M. Hubble, B. Duncan and S. Miller (eds) *The Heart and Soul of Change: What Works in Therapy.* Washington: American Psychological Association.

Peacock, F. (2001) *Water the Flowers, Not the Weeds.* Montreal: Open Heart Publishing.

Pinker, S. (1997) *How the Mind Works.* London: Allen Lane.

Pinker, S. (1999) *Words and Rules.* London: Weidenfeld & Nicolson.

Pinker, S. (2002) *The Blank Slate: The Modern Denial of Human Nature.* London: Penguin Books.

Pruitt, J. and Rubin, D. (1993) *Social Conflict: Escalation, Stalemate and Settlement.* New York: McGraw-Hill.

Rafi, F., Oskouie, F. and Mansoure, M. (2004) 'Factors involved in nurses' responses to burnout: a grounded theory study.' *BMC Nursing 3,* 6. Available at www.biomedcentral.com/1472-6955/3/6, accessed on 14 August 2010.

Rheingold, H. (1988) *They Have a Word for IT: A Lighthearted Lexicon of Untranslatable Words and Phrases.* Los Angeles, CA: Jeremy P. Tarcher.

Richardson, J. (1988) *The Magic of Rapport: How You Can Gain Personal Power in Any Situation.* Capitola, CA: Meta Publications.

Rogers, C. (1967) *On Becoming a Person: A Therapist's View of Psychotherapy.* London: Constable.

Rossi, E. L. (1986) *The Psychobiology of Mind-Body Healing: New Concepts of Therapeutic Hypnosis.* London: W.W. Norton.

Satir, V. (1988) *The New Peoplemaking.* Mountain View, CA: Science and Behavior Books.

Schaap, C., Bennun, I., Schindler, L. and Hoogduin, K. (1993) *The Therapeutic Relationship in Behavioural Therapy.* Chichester: Wiley.

Seligman, M. (1995) *Learned Optimism: How to Change Your Mind and Your Life.* New York: Simon & Schuster.

Seligman, M. (1998) 'Why therapy works.' *APA Monitor 29,* 12.

Seligman, M. (2003) *Authentic Happiness: Using the New Positive Psychology to Realise Your Potential for Lasting Fulfillment.* London: Nicholas Brealey.

Senge, P. (2006) *The Fifth Discipline: The Art and Practice of the Learning Organisation.* London: Random House.

Shapiro, A. (1959) 'The placebo effect in the history of medical treatment: Implications for psychiatry.' *American Journal of Psychiatry 116,* 298–304.

Snyder, C., Michael, S. and Cheavens, J. (2001) 'Hope as a psychotherapeutic foundation of common factors, placebos and expectancies.' In M. Hubble, B. Duncan and S. Miller (eds) *The Heart and Soul of Change.* Washington, DC: APA.

Stack Sullivan, H. (1970) *The Psychiatric Interview.* New York: W.W. Norton.

Street, E. and Downey, J. (1996) *Brief Therapeutic Consultations: An Approach to Systemic Counselling.* London: Wiley.

Symynkywicz, J. (1991) 'Vaclav Havel and the politics of hope.' *Neotic Sciences Review 18,* 21–26.

Tallman, K. and Bohart, A. (2001) *The Client as a Common Factor: Clients as Self-Healers.* In M. Hubble, B. Duncan and S. Miller (eds) *The Heart and Soul of Change: What Works in Therapy.* Washington: American Psychological Association.

Talmon, M. (1990) *Single Session Therapy: Maximising the Effect of the First (and Often Only) Therapeutic Encounter.* San Francisco, CA: Jossey-Bass.

Thorana, N. and Frank, T. (2007) *Handbook of Solution-Focused Brief Therapy: Clinical Applications.* London: Routledge.

Tomm, K. (1987) 'Interventive interviewing: Part 2. Reflexive questioning as a means of enabling self-healing.' *Family Process 26,* 2, 167–183.

Tomm, K. (1989) 'Externalizing the problem and internalizing personal agency.' *Journal of Strategic and Systemic Therapies 8,* 1, 16–22.

Tonge, W.L. (1967) 'Listening with the third ear.' *Journal of the Royal College of General Practitioners 13* (suppl. 3), 13–17.

Turnell, A. and Edwards, S. (1999) *Signs of Safety: A Solution Focused Approach to Child Protection Casework.* New York: W.W. Norton.

Walter, J. and Peller, J. (1992) *Becoming Solution Focused in Brief Therapy.* Levittown, PA: Brunner Mazel.

Wampold, B. (2001) *The Great Psychotherapy Debate: Models, Methods and Findings.* Mahwah, NJ: Laurence Earlbaum Associates.

Watzlawick, P. (1978) *The Language of Change.* New York: W.W. Norton.

Watzlawick, P. and Weakland, J. (eds) (1977) *The Interactional View: Studies at the Mental Research Institute Palo Alto 1965–74.* New York: W.W. Norton.

Watzlawick, P., Weakland, J. and Fisch, R. (1974) *Change: Principles of Problem Formation and Problem Resolution.* New York: W.W. Norton.

White, M. and Epston, D. (1990) *Narrative Means to Therapeutic Ends.* New York: W.W. Norton.

Winbolt, B. (1996) 'Bill O'Hanlon: Open to possibilities.' *The Therapist 3,* 4, 36–40.

Yalom, I. (1989) *Love's Executioner and Other Tales of Psychotherapy.* London: Penguin Books.

Yalom, I. (2003) *An Interview with Insoo Kim Berg.* Available at www.Psychotherapy.net/interview/Insoo_Kim_Berg, accessed on 14 August 2010.

Yapko, M. (1992) *Hypnosis and the Treatment of Depressions: Strategies for Change.* Levittown, PA: Brunner Mazel.

Zeig, J. and Munion, M. (1999) *Milton H. Erickson.* New York: Sage.

Further Reading

The following are suggestions for reading on SFBT relating to specific areas:

General

Berg, I. and Dolan, Y. (2001) *Tales of Solutions: A Collection of Hope Inspiring Stories*. New York: W.W. Norton.

O'Hanlon, W. and Weiner-Davis, M. (1989) *In Search of Solutions: A New Direction in Psychotherapy*. New York: W.W. Norton.

Walter, J. and Peller, J. (1992) *Becoming Solution Focused in Brief Therapy*. Levittown, PA: Brunner Mazel.

Alcohol abuse

Berg, I. and Miller, S. (1992) *Working with the Problem Drinker: A Solution-Focused Approach*. New York: W.W. Norton.

Child protection

Turnell, A. and Edwards, S. (1999) *Signs of Safety: A Solution Focused Approach to Child Protection Casework*. New York: W.W. Norton.

Education

Rhodes, J. and Ajmal, Y. (1995) *Solution Focused Thinking in Schools: Behaviour, Reading and Organisation*. London: BT Press.

Groups

Sharry, J. (2007) *Solution-Focused Groupwork* (2nd edition). London: Sage Publications Ltd.

Suicide

Henden, J. (2008) *Preventing Suicide: The Solution Focused Approach*. Chichester: Wiley and Sons.

Subject Index

Author Index